Logra Tu Dream

"How 50 Successful Latinos & Latinas Turned Their Dreams Into Reality"

ARTURO NAVA

i

PRAISE FOR THE LOGRA TU DREAM BOOK

"This book highlights the tremendous accomplishment that Latinos are capable of through inspiring stories of some of the most successful Hispanic leaders and entrepreneurs in this country. It demonstrates without a doubt that it is possible for anybody in our community to achieve their highest aspirations if they embrace the mindset of success, work very hard and take action in pursuit of their dreams."

- Manny Ruiz, Founder Hispanicize

"Look for inspiration from those who have walked their talk. Arturo Nava's Logra Tu Dream book is the real deal. He started walking in that path with less than $300. This book gives concrete examples of how the talented and determined have changed the world as we know it. Thanks to the pioneers he featured in this book, this country has new products, services and experiences. I am grateful that Arturo has had the foresight and vision to capture our knowledge and collective wisdom. Felicidades."

- Deldelp Medina, Founder and CEO Avion Ventures

"A Vital tool for any young Latino trying to make it! Thank you for your Book. I started reading it and couldn't put it down. I needed something like this. As a first generation Mexican-American these types of resources are what we lack in our community. Even with an MBA I need guidance in a number of topics from the minor details of starting a business to simply reading how others did it. Hope you do start a mastermind and I hope I can be part of it."

- Conrado Flores, reader and Amazon book reviewer

2

"Within the pages of this book and the selfless act of kindness and leadership, Arturo Nava provides others the guidance to navigate through overcoming seemingly impossible obstacles to succeed at multiple levels in your life."

- Robert Renteria, Author of From The Barrio to The Boardroom & Civic Leader

"This book is a much needed roadmap for millions of Latinos and Latinas who work incredibly hard every day to give their families a better future. It will inspire you to take action to pursue your highest aspirations and provide you with the same tools that some of the most successful among us have used to achieve success. Logra Tu Dream is a call to action that will motivate the Latino community to reach its tremendous potential !!"

-Lizza Monet Morales, top Latina influencer, actress, TV host and content creator

"A Blueprint for Success. This book is a classic must have for anyone seeking to create a better life for themselves. Success leaves clues and Arturo was able to capture the step by step guidance in a very easy and actionable manner that you can apply immediately in your lives. Read a chapter or open up a page and you will be inspired and on path to achieve your BIG dreams. Thank you, Arturo for taking the time to share your wisdom. You are a gem!"

- Deborah Deras, entrepreneur, life coach and speaker

"Logra Tu Dream reminds us that it is vital for our community to keep embracing a Si Se Puede attitude and to develop our full potential both individually and collectively."

-Gaby Natale, President Super Latina TV

"Best book ever about successful Latino entrepreneurs, unveils the stories of the people that started from very humble beginnings to successful enterprises; immigrants that had many obstacles in this country and how they achieved their American dream. Arturo recognizes that the lack of mentorship and the "sí, se puede" (it is possible) mindset needs to be really adopted by those of us seeking our dream. This book will teach you the roadmap to success, and help you avoid costly mistakes that others made. I really encourage you to read this book and learn from the best Latino entrepreneurs. Arturo thank you for your hard work and dedication to the Latino community, you are truly an inspiration to me. Sí, se puede!"

- Felipe Diaz, reader and Amazon book reviewer

"Great blend of inspiration and actionable advice! This book is one part inspiration and one part instruction manual for success in life. Although I am not a Latino, I found the principles, resources, and action steps to be practical and on target for not just becoming a successful person, but also for becoming a better person. Every young person who thinks the odds are stacked against him or her or anyone who simply doesn't have a clue of how to pursue the American Dream should read this book!"

- Mark N. Tuggle, reader and Amazon book reviewer

ISBN-13:978-0692533734 (Logra Tu Dream Publishing)

ISBN-10:0692533737

DISCLAIMER

Although the author and publisher have made every effort to ensure that the information in this book was correct at press time, the author and publisher do not assume and hereby disclaim any liability to any party for any loss, damage, or disruption caused by errors or omissions, whether such errors or omissions result from negligence, accident, or any other cause.

This book is intended for informational purposes only. This book includes information, products, and services by third parties. These Third Party Materials consist of products and opinions expressed by their owners. As such, the author does not assume responsibility or liability for any Third Party material or opinions. The publication of such Third Party Materials does not constitute the author's guarantee of any information, instruction, opinion, products, or services contained within the Third Party Material. The use of recommended Third Party Material does not guarantee any success and/or earnings related to you or your business.

Publication of such Third Party Material is simply a recommendation and an expression of the author's own opinion of that material. Links to Third Party Resources may be affiliate links, meaning the author may receive compensation if a service is ultimately purchased from such a link. No part of this publication shall be reproduced, transmitted, or sold in whole or in part in any form, without the prior written consent of the author. All trademarks and registered trademarks appearing in this book are the property of their respective owners.

Users of this guide are advised to do their own due diligence when it comes to making business decisions and all information, products, and services that have been provided should be independently verified by your own qualified professionals. By reading this guide, you agree that the author is not responsible for the success or failure of your business decisions relating to any information presented in this book. ©2015 Arturo Nava.

DEDICATIONS

To my precious children, Arturo and Veronica, who are the light of my life, so that they are inspired to dream big and turn their dreams into reality.

To my mother Maria Antonieta, who is my eternal supporter and who taught me to persevere, to enjoy life to the fullest, and to pursue the life of my dreams with passion and courage.

To my late father Arturo Antonio, who is my hero and who taught me to keep the fire in my belly burning so that I could achieve my dreams.

To my girlfriend Gina, who keeps me grounded and who has been there for me in the good times and the bad times.

To my Aunt Nina and my sister Maria Antonieta, who helped me when I most needed it, making it possible for me to come to the US to pursue my dreams.

To my late uncle Francisco Chavez (Panchito) who showed me that our kindness of heart and joy for living is what will live on in the hearts of those whose lives we touch.

TABLE OF CONTENTS

ACKNOWLEDGEMENTS

I would like to express my deepest gratitude to all of the people who made this book possible. In life nothing of significance can be achieved alone and this book is no different...

First of all, thank you to the 54 million hardworking and brave Latinos & Latinas living in this country for inspiring me to start Logra Tu Dream and write this book.

To the more than 50 inspiring Latinos, Latinas and Latin-inspired entrepreneurs and leaders for sharing your stories and mentorship on the Logra Tu Dream podcast, which made this book possible.

To all the fantastic authors at the Self Publishing School for providing me the guidance, motivation and structure to help me make this dream a reality.

To my editor, Beth Balmanno for helping me turn my rough drafts into a well-written book, and for sharing invaluable advice with me.

To the super talented Juan Correa for designing a wonderful cover for this book.

To Gaby Natale, an incredibly inspiring and kind Latina entrepreneur, for writing the forward for this book.

To Eddie Torres for recording my audio book with boundless patience.

To my dad for planting the seed many years ago to come to this country to pursue my dream.

To my girlfriend Gina, my mother, my sister and my children for your support, patience and excitement throughout this journey.

FOREWORD

What do Latinos who achieve exceptional success in the United States have in common? Is there a certain mindset that helped them reach their goals? If so, can it be summarized and replicated?

This is the question stated by Arturo Nava in "Logra Tu Dream", a book that explores the principles behind 50 success stories of self-made Hispanic leaders. From White House officials to tech innovators to millionaire entrepreneurs, these men and women show that it takes blood, sweat, tears -and *ganas!*- to overcome the odds and be a part of the American Dream.

As Latinos continue to shape the identity and future of the United States, "Logra Tu Dream" reminds us that it is vital for our community to keep embracing a *Si Se Puede* attitude and to develop our full potential both individually and collectively.

"Logra Tu Dream" is also Arturo's personal story: an incredible journey that transforms a humble kid from Mexico City with no money and no connections into a Harvard graduate and successful entrepreneur.

Arturo's no-nonsense approach to personal growth is a useful resource for *soñadores* at all stages in life. From the teenager who is planning to go to college and worries about student loan debt.

To the corporate executive who wants to reinvent himself and start his own business. To the retired professional who

13

had an outstanding career but is looking for a sense of purpose and ways to give back to the community.

Get ready to learn and be inspired.

Who knows? You could be the story number 51 ;).

Gaby Natale, President Super Latina TV

Chapter 1

INTRODUCTION

What do the founder of Hispanicize, the president of Super Latina TV, the chief of staff of the White House Initiative for Educational Excellence for Hispanics, the former president of Telemundo, and the founder of the largest voiceover marketplace in the world have in common? They all are Latinos and Latinas that have turned their dreams into reality.

They also all (consciously or not) used a set of principles to achieve their success. I know this because I interviewed them on my Logra Tu Dream podcast. I learned how 50 of the most successful Latinos and Latinas in this country are achieving their dreams.

There has never been so much opportunity for anyone with the desire and drive to achieve their American Dream. Advances in technology create new opportunities in the marketplace every day for those that know how to capitalize on them. Yet achieving the American Dream has also become increasingly difficult for many Latinos despite the huge opportunities.

The dream has become more elusive because there is a lack of mentorship and inspiration from Latino and Latina role models who demonstrate that "si se puede" (it is possible) and who share their roadmap to success.

People don't believe they can make their dreams reality because they are not surrounded by people who have shown them it is possible.

Unfortunately, we don't have enough role models demonstrating how to achieve our dreams and providing the needed mentorship to millions of Latinos and Latinas trying to find their way in life.

But there is a book that will show you how 50 successful Latinos and Latinas turned their dreams into reality. It will lay out the 12 proven principles that have propelled these Latino entrepreneurs and leaders to their success in an easy to understand way. This book will show you that *your* dream is possible if you learn and put into action the proven principles you discover here.

The Logra Tu Dream book has synthesized the mindset, actions and habits that have propelled these 50+ Latino & Latina role models to their success in an easy to read and concise manner. This book is for all of you out there who have a dream and the drive to pursue it but who haven't found the way. This book is for those who don't believe that "si se puede" (you can make it), for those that might be about to lose hope and let go of their dreams.

Eighteen years ago, I emigrated from Mexico to the US to pursue my own American Dream of building a better future for myself, and to start my own family. In those 18 years I have been deeply inspired by the stories, struggles and triumphs of many Latinos and their children who are pursuing their dreams of a better life for their families in the US.

Many times, I saw a lack of access to inspiration, mentorship, business advice, as well as tools from successful Latino role models, standing in the way of their dreams. I looked for roadmaps but I didn't find any.

I realized that my mission is to do my part to help other Latinos achieve their dreams of securing a better future for their families and growing their entrepreneurial businesses.

To do this, I needed to give a voice to the stories of Latino & Latina role models, to inspire, mentor and provide business advice, and most importantly, to show all of my fellow Latinos & Latinas that have doubted whether they can achieve their dreams that "Si Se Puede."

I set out to find how the most accomplished Latinos and Latinas were achieving their success. What were they doing differently? How they were thinking differently?

This is why I decided to start the "Logra Tu Dream" podcast, in which successful Latino and Latin-inspired entrepreneurs and leaders share their journeys in making their American Dreams a reality.

Over the last year I interviewed more than 50 of the most successful Latinos and Latinas in America. They have shared their stories and provided insight into the mindset, actions and habits that allowed them to overcome barriers and conquer fears, which have propelled them to achieve what they once thought impossible.

These inspirational people have become some of the most successful entrepreneurs, leaders, influencers, executives and artists in the Latino community by adopting the principles you will read about in this book.

Robert Renteria grew up in the barrio, overcoming a very difficult upbringing and escaping the gangs to become a successful businessman. He is the international best-selling author of the book series, *From the Barrio to the Boardroom,* and a keynote speaker.

Manny Ruiz saw a need and filled the gap, starting and building Hispanicize into the most influential event in the Latino world for content creators, marketers, artists and journalists.

Jackie Camacho beat cancer twice and rose from humble beginnings to become a successful entrepreneur, speaker, and seven-time author by the age of 32.

What do these three people have in common?

They all achieved the seemingly impossible by implementing the mindset, habits and actions that you will read about in this book.

I promise that if you follow the system in this book, it will accelerate your journey to achieve your dream. You will save years of your life and avoid costly mistakes that can and will set you back.

As Warren Buffett said, *"You learn by mistakes, but they don't have to be yours."* I promise that you will be inspired and that you will believe it is possible for you to live the life of success and secure the happiness you envision.

Don't be the person who misses out on opportunities to take your life where you want to because you don't learn from people who have achieved what you want to achieve. Be the person other people admire and want to emulate. Be the person other people see and say, "I want to follow their footsteps." Be the person who takes massive action and does so immediately.

The mindset, actions and habits of successful Latinos and Latinas you're about to read have been proven to help many achieve "La Buena Vida" (the good life), one filled with health, wealth, happiness, and familia. All you have to do to understand the system to achieve your dream is to keep reading. Each chapter will walk you through each of the 12 principles of this success system and will inspire you to dream big and to take action.

This book starts with my story and an overview on the Latino American Dream. If you are the type of person who wants to skip the background and "cut to the chase", you can go straight to the 12 principles starting with the chapter on "Believe that si se puede".

Of course if after reading the principles, you want to go back to learn more about my story, about why I started the Logra Tu Dream platform and about research on the Latino American Dream it will give you more context. The choice is yours as to where to begin.

Take control of your mindset right now. Take massive action, turn your actions into habits, keep the fire in your belly burning, and you will Logra Tu Dream!!

Chapter 2

MY STORY

I am Arturo Nava, the father of two precious kids, a Mexican immigrant, founder of the "Logra Tu Dream" podcast, brand marketer, and a student and lover of life.

My biggest blessings are my two precious kids, my loving girlfriend, my close-knit family, my good friends, and my good health. My dream is to help others achieve their dreams and to live "La Buena Vida." "La Buena Vida" for me is one filled with the love of family, freedom to live your purpose, passion, inspiration, great Mexican food, and happy memorable moments.

"La Buena Vida" is my definition of a wealthy life. It obviously implies having the financial resources to be free to live the life that I want, but the financial aspect is only a limited part of my definition of wealth.

I was born and raised in Mexico City in a loving, middle-class family. I grew up in the 70s and 80s during a time of intense change. From the VCR, the cell phone and the Internet to smart phones and today's technological world — in the last 40+ years, the world has become smaller and much more complex.

I was very fortunate to have been born in Mexico, a wonderful country with a deep soul and a passion for life, along with amazing culture, food, and people. In Mexico bonds are deep, good friends are lifelong, and life is a celebration. Mexico has left a deep imprint in my heart; I will always love my "Mexico Lindo."

My mother, Maria Antonieta Correa Campos, is passionate, bold, and an entrepreneurial free spirit. She taught me to be brave, to persevere and to enjoy life to the fullest. My mother has incredible persuasion powers and never gives up; this skill has served her well throughout her life to get what she wants.

She has always been an entrepreneur: she sold office supplies growing up and then took up the hardware business of her second husband. When he suddenly died in 1992, she had to take full responsibility of the business to be able to make a living. She struggled mightily through lean years but persevered, working hard to re-build her life. She kept herself busy and healthy, and was always there for my sister and me.

Today she is able to live an enviable life with her partner of 20 years, spending her days in the company of many great friends at the German Club, a sports and social club in Mexico she visits frequently. She spends time with her grandchildren, reads, and enjoys activities with family and friends.

From her I learned to follow my dreams without fears and to persevere in the face of the worst adversity.

My father, Arturo A. Nava Regazzoni, who passed away in 2003, was a brilliant self-made man who inspired and challenged me to reach my full potential. He was a mechanical engineer, first in his class in college at the Iberoamerican University in Mexico City. He was the president of the student council in college and a pioneer in the computer industry in Mexico.

He grew up without a dad and rose from humble beginnings to become a top executive in his field. He loved computers and always knew what he wanted, and his work ethic was admirable. He believed in always doing the best job you can.

He taught me that you can achieve your dreams with hard work, discipline and vision. One day, a few months before he died, I asked him how I could achieve my dreams.

He said, "Mijo, always keep the fire in your belly burning and you will achieve your dream." When I asked him about the secret to his success he answered, "I broke down my goals into smaller, manageable goals I could achieve." These two teachings from my father have inspired me and helped me immensely to overcome obstacles and attain a better life for myself and my family.

This is a picture of me with my mom, dad and sister many years ago when I was a kid

24

The American Dream captured my imagination from an early age. I grew up with a strong American influence around me. Growing up, I loved watching NFL football, and I became a lifelong fan of the Pittsburg Steelers. I loved American movies, from *Star Wars* to *Rocky*, and from *ET* to *St. Elmo's Fire*.

I loved the American toys, gadgets, and candies my father would bring back to me from his travels to the US. I was fortunate enough to be able to visit Disneyland and Disneyworld as a kid and experience the US. At the age of 12, I came to Ashfield, Massachusetts as an exchange student for a month. I experienced life as an American kid and I loved it.

But what most fascinated me about the US were the stories of Americans who were able to achieve their dreams regardless of their family background, financial situation, race, or country of origin. These stories proved to me many times that anything is possible in this country.

In Mexico, I grew keenly aware of the huge inequality in society and how socio-economic status was a key driver of success. Being born into the right family and having the right connections provides people a huge advantage in any society as it relates to their ability to become successful.

But in Mexico this advantage for the most fortunate seemed to be much larger, which made it much harder for people coming from modest means to achieve their dreams. It always bothered me that in Mexico there never seemed to be equal opportunity.

Public education was very poor, so if your family could not pay for a private school you would be at a huge disadvantage when trying to get into a good college. The best colleges are private so the cycle of exclusion reinforces itself. When it came to careers, the good jobs were reserved for the well connected and well-educated.

Until recently, the barriers to entrepreneurship were pretty high, too. I always rebelled against the oligarchic social structures that I experienced in Mexico. I knew that if I were to live in Mexico, I would dedicate my life to changing this structure.

But the only way to change the system in Mexico, I thought, was to change the corrupt political system from within. I would probably have been a very unsuccessful Mexican politician, as I believe in fairness, honesty and equal opportunity. Not exactly the qualities of successful Mexican politicians.

So was I to become a Mexican politician and compromise my ideals? Of course not. For a brief period of time, I thought that maybe I could craft myself an independent political career, but with time I realized this was not my calling.

At my core, I have always resonated deeply with the American ideal that everybody is created equal and that anyone can achieve their American Dream through hard work. This is why I decided early on that I wanted to come to the US and pursue my own American Dream.

When I was 12 years old, my father brought me back a duffel bag with the Harvard logo. He'd gone to Boston on a business trip and he told me how Harvard was one of the best universities in the world, and that he'd enjoyed visiting it. That day I told my dad that one day I would go to Harvard. Of course, he laughed. But from that moment on, I was committed to working on my dream to come to the US and go to Harvard.

So I worked hard at school and got into a good college. Even though I knew I wanted to have a strong impact on other peoples' lives, I was lost, as I didn't know what I wanted to study or what I was good at. My father urged me to study something useful like engineering or business.

I was so lost that I didn't listen. I enrolled in economics but after only six months I decided it was not for me. I changed to International Relations and, while I did enjoy some classes on political theory, I found that what I was learning was not practical knowledge I could apply to most jobs.

So I changed again, this time to Business Administration. And this time, I stuck to it. My mother's second husband had just died and I needed to find a job to support myself and pay for my expenses.

I also had promised myself that I would do everything in my power to come to the US to do my MBA. My goal was to go to Harvard so I worked hard at school and I got involved in extracurricular leadership activities.

I got a good job as a financial trader during college, and I prepared for a year for the GMAT, taking courses after work. I worked on my essays for more than a year and I spent my weekends studying for the GMAT.

I applied to a number of MBA programs and applied for a scholarship. Harvard was the only school who offered me a phone interview; I called and asked if it was possible to do a live interview. They said yes, so I flew myself to Boston and prepared for three days in the hotel room for the interview. This was my golden opportunity and I would do everything in my power to seize it.

My ticket to my new life in the US came via my acceptance to the MBA program at Harvard. A few weeks after my interview in Boston, I received a UPS notice at my home in Mexico. I flew to the UPS office just before it closed. I couldn't believe my fortune when I saw the fat envelope from Harvard with acceptance materials and a letter that read, "I am pleased to inform you that you have been accepted to the Harvard Business School..."

I had been accepted to the Harvard Business School! My dream of going to Harvard, the dream I'd told my father about 14 years earlier, was now a reality. With the acceptance in hand, I won a scholarship from the Mexican government that made it possible for me to attend.

My two years at Harvard were life-changing, stimulating and challenging. I was humbled to be in such great company with the most successful and promising young business leaders of my generation. I could not believe I was now among them.

I grew personally and professionally like never before, and I was exposed to the latest thinking in business. I studied harder than ever, I made good friends, and I attended as many activities as I could. Stimulation surrounded me, as did great people and amazing opportunities.

It was a world filled with great choices on countless career paths. In such a world, my biggest problem was how to choose the best path for me. I wanted to capitalize on all the opportunities, but I knew I couldn't. Making a choice was very difficult. I didn't want to narrow my choices until I knew what I wanted to do in my life, but this, my friends, is a tough question to answer when you are young.

It takes years of experimentation and trial and error to find yourself, many times over. This is why mentorship is so important; a great mentor can save you years of searching for your calling.

I had been counseled by my dad and by a college professor, but at that point in my life, I needed a mentor. But I was naïve and didn't understand the importance of having one. So instead I started off my career, running straight into a wall, a wall that would teach me many lessons that would help me tremendously but that could have been avoided.

My aspirations grew during my MBA education. I could not wait to get out into the world and to make my mark. After my MBA, I started off my US adventure as an entrepreneur. My first venture, itradefood.com, didn't work out. I struggled mightily with this endeavor; I went six months without a salary, trying to raise money. I finally was able to find investors but made critical mistakes that would ultimately lead to failure.

I went into a market that seemed huge on paper but which had not been validated as a viable business opportunity. It was the early wild, Wild West days of the Internet. My B2B business for international trade of food between the US and Mexico was too early for its time.

My choice of team members and partner was not the best, either. Itradefood was a failure and it had cost me two years of my life. I was going to start over, but now saddled with debt and newly married. The stress level was very high and I realized I needed to learn a craft to become valuable to the marketplace.

My Harvard MBA was a great asset. It opened doors but I needed to pick a niche and build skills if I wanted to achieve success. I decided that marketing was my niche; I had always been good at marketing assignments in school. Conceptual, big picture thinking came as second nature to me, and in my startup experience, marketing had been what I enjoyed the most.

So I looked for a job in marketing and found my start at P&G, a fantastic marketing school. I worked for the big brands for 13 years in various brand marketing and innovation leadership roles, growing top brands at companies like Procter & Gamble, Molson Coors/Miller Coors, and Google-Motorola.

From my experience working for big brands, I learned how to build a brand. I learned how to lead teams and discovered my passion for building brands in the Latino market. Most importantly, I got to know myself better.

I discovered that, while I loved strategy and building brands and was very good at it, I didn't enjoy the politics and bureaucracy of big companies. I was fortunate to have had a couple of good mentors who helped me grow my career and navigate the corporate waters.

After 13 years building brands for big companies, I discovered my strengths: I realized that I excelled at thinking strategically and was very passionate about my work. I realized it was easy and fun for me to come up with ideas, putting all the dots together to grow brands. I had become an expert in helping companies grow their businesses in the Latino market and I loved it.

I have had a lot of success helping brands like Coors Light grow in the Latino market and launching new brands/products as I did with Nuestro Yogurt.

But I also realized I was better suited and would be much happier and successful doing so in smaller, more entrepreneurial environments. After all, I always found myself thinking and acting like an entrepreneur in the big companies I worked for.

I took the entrepreneurial plunge for the second time in 2012, after I was laid off from Motorola, when they decided to eliminate their marketing department after they were acquired by Google. I started Marketealo; a consulting firm that helped companies win in the Latino and Latin-influenced market.

Most recently, I have been working at Nuestro Queso, an entrepreneurial Hispanic dairy products company in

Chicago. I am enjoying building the Nuestro Queso brand, launching Nuestro Yogurt while I also support my community. I have built my platform based on the idea that to attract and retain loyal Latina customers, you need to give first.

Brands need to add value to people's lives to capture their hearts and be in their minds. "Give and you shall receive." The days of pushing brands with advertising and not giving are over, in my humble opinion, and the term 'marketing' is outdated. I now think of myself more as a brand builder and advocate for the community I serve rather than as a marketer.

It was clear that I was starting to find myself when I first started working with the Latino market. I felt intense passion for the work and a sense of mission. But I wanted to help my people, not just market to them, so I started thinking about writing a book about the stories of other Latinos trying to achieve their dreams.

I didn't get around to it. I was too immersed in a mindset of having a job and then going home and enjoying my family. I didn't pursue any other projects outside of work; I didn't meet enough new people. I was comfortable with my job but I was unsatisfied. I knew I was not working towards fulfilling my purpose. I was making a good living but was not having the impact I wanted to have.

But in the last 12 years, life dealt me a couple of hard blows that made me realize the fragility of life. Everything can disappear, without notice. When they happened, they seemed like insurmountable setbacks in my life, but in fact they provided the fuel that rekindled the fire inside of me to pursue my mission.

In 2003, my father passed away from lung cancer after an 18-month battle with the disease. This was a profound and devastating loss for me. I felt as if somebody had ripped my heart out with their bare hands. I loved my father with all my heart; he was my hero and not having him in my life anymore left a deep hole.

Before he was diagnosed with cancer, he looked as healthy as could be and younger than his age, sporting only a few gray hairs in his late fifties. He was vibrant and full of energy and ideas. Sadly, in only a few months, cancer took all that away, including his life.

The second big blow came in 2009, when my then-wife told me she wanted a divorce while on a trip she took to visit her father in Florida with my kids. My dreams of growing old with my family, and being able to see my children every day of their childhood, disappeared in a moment.

I have always been a great father and had been a good husband, too. I felt that my ex-wife and I had grown apart emotionally but I had been willing to stick it out for the sake of being a family and being able to give my kids a childhood with both of their parents.

So I was shocked and saddened that this would happen to me. I immensely enjoyed life as a dad to my two precious children, and nothing hurt me more than the thought that now as a divorced dad, I could not live with my kids full time. Through the divorce process I tried to get my kids back to California, but it was impossible. They stayed in Florida and then moved to Dallas with their mom.

I moved to Chicago for a job while the divorce took its course. I figured I would be better off in Chicago until they settled in a city so that I would not move to somewhere they would later leave. Since then, I have traveled to see my kids every two weeks, and I Skype with them every single day.

I bring them to Chicago in the summer and devote all the time off I have to being with them. It is not ideal but we have a wonderful relationship and I have spent significant quality time with them over the last six years.

My kids feel loved and feel that I am a big presence in their lives; they are very happy and that is what matters. I cherish each moment I have with them and I am grateful that God blessed me with such precious children.

For the second time in only a few years, two precious aspects of my life were taken away. First it was my father and then it was my dream of having a traditional family in which you see your kids grow up in the family home.

This second blow woke me up to the reality that if I didn't take immediate action to fulfill my calling, I might not have the opportunity later on. I didn't want to die with my music inside of me. These setbacks became the kick in the pants I needed from life to truly pursue my dreams without fears or limitations.

I now understood how precious the moments of happiness and abundance in life are. I felt a deep urge to savor life fully and not let the fire I had inside me die. This is the fire of my life calling, of my highest aspirations. I decided to feed this fire, as I knew it would help me create the life of my dreams.

Why I started the Logra Tu Dream podcast

As I mentioned, I've long wanted to write a book about the American dreams of Latinos in the US. For the reasons I explained, I never got around to it. But the idea and the passion for someday doing something about this never left me.

I had a deep desire to tell the untold stories of Latino success in America so that they could inspire others to reach for their dreams. So I started the Logra Tu Dream podcast and platform in April, 2014. I did it from scratch, being a total newbie to podcasting.

Logra Tu Dream podcast guests up to about 7/2015

The Inspiration

After living for 18 years in the US, I have been deeply inspired by the stories, the struggles, and the triumphs of many Latinos and Latinas and their children who are pursuing their dreams of creating a better life for their families. These brave Latinos and Latinas have made immense sacrifices, leaving their mothers, fathers and sometimes their children behind in their home countries in order to pursue better opportunities in the US so that they can give their families a better future.

They are heroes who are willing to endure the separation from the people they love most in the world and to work harder than anybody on the most difficult jobs in order to achieve their dreams of giving their families a better life.

Yet I saw that many times, standing in the way of their dreams was a lack of access to inspiration, mentorship, business advice and tools from successful Latino and Latin-inspired role models.

I have realized that my mission is to do my part in helping other Latinos achieve their dreams of securing a better future for their families and growing their entrepreneurial businesses.

This is why I decided to start the "Logra Tu Dream" podcast, in which successful Latino and Latin-inspired entrepreneurs and leaders share their journeys to making their American dreams a reality.

As a Mexican immigrant who came to the US in pursuit of my own American dream, I know well how inspiration, mentorship, and business advice from successful role models can go a long way to empower thousands of Latinos in the US and beyond.

I started listening to podcasts in 2012; sometime in 2013 I started listening to John Lee Dumas' Entrepreneur on Fire podcast. I was incredibly inspired by John and the stories of his guests—top entrepreneurs who have overcome failures to achieve fantastic success. I couldn't get enough of the podcasts.

At the time, I had just started Marketealo, my consulting company focused on helping companies navigate and win in the Latin-influenced market through innovation, brand development, and strategic marketing.

I realized that podcasting was the perfect medium to accomplish the mission. This is how the idea of Logra Tu Dream was born.

Just to say thanks for buying and reading my book, I would like to give you the Audiobook version 100% FREE! Go to: www.logratudream.com/freeaudiobook

Chapter 3

THE LATINO AMERICAN DREAM

"What do Latinos who achieve exceptional success in the United States have in common? Is there a certain mindset that helped them reach their goals? If so, can it be summarized and replicated? From White House officials to tech innovators to millionaire entrepreneurs, these men and women show that it takes blood, sweat, tears -and ganas!- to overcome the odds and be a part of the American Dream."

- Gaby Natale, President Super Latina TV

Over the last 18 years that I have lived here in the US, I have talked to many Latinos and Latinas about their dreams and their journeys to pursue these dreams. I learned about their aspirations and the barriers that stood in their way.

There are 54 million Latinos living in the US, and we believe deeply in the American dream. Our parents and grandparents came to this country in pursuit of it and we have followed in their footsteps.

We left our countries and our families to seek a better life for ourselves and for the same families we left. We arrived with big dreams and a willingness to work as hard as humanly possible. We have started new families in this land, we have adopted many things from this culture, and we have adapted to the American way of life. But we keep and cherish our culture.

Our mindset is more American than before but our heart remains Latino.

In fact, according to research, we are more optimistic than non-Latinos as it relates to our belief in being able to achieve our dreams. And these dreams of ours are different than non-Latinos.

Again and again, I heard that your dream revolves around securing a better future for your families, building your entrepreneurial business, and controlling your own destiny. But always at the core of the American dream of Latinos was the future of their families. They told me that providing a better future for their families was the biggest reason why they work so hard to succeed in this country.

We dream about owning our own home and about leaving our kids enough money so that they don't have to worry about money. We dream about providing our kids a better education than we had.

According to a study on the pursuit of the American dream among business owners[1], the major motivations of Latinos to start their businesses were to pursue the American Dream, to take control of their lives, and to support their families.

Reasons For Owning a Business		
Reason	National	Hispanic
Provide financially for family	77%	89%
Be own boss	57%	79%
Have more control of life, time, etc.	53%	76%
Have strong passion for craft or trade	47%	61%
To follow your dreams	36%	66%
Something tangible to pass on to children	35%	55%
Only way to get ahead	32%	60%
Give back to the community	21%	54%
Provide jobs for other family members	19%	31%
Other family members wanted to start business, so joined them	18%	26%

Eighty-nine percent of Latino entrepreneurs start a business to provide financially for their families. Seventy-nine percent start a business to be their own boss versus 57 percent for all business owners. Seventy-six percent start a business to have more control over their lives and time versus 53 percent for all business owners.

Fifty-five percent start a business to have something tangible to pass on to their children, versus 35 percent for all business owners. Thirty-one percent wanted to provide jobs for other family members, versus 19 percent generally.

Sixty-six percent start a business to follow their dreams versus 36 percent for all business owners.

It is very clear that we have a deep desire to control our own destinies and secure our family's future. Being able to take control of our lives means having the wealth, time, and freedom to enjoy our families. Also it is clear that we start our own business to pursue our dreams much more so than non-Latinos.

Our optimism and desire to pursue our dreams like our entrepreneurial inclinations are undeniable. We work very hard to fund the education of our kids, and we believe in giving back and supporting our parents financially. We try to avoid debt as much as possible; we want to save for retirement and get rid of the debt that we have.

Many of us have worked around the clock to put food on the table or have seen our parents do so. We have struggled; we have had to figure out how to survive in a new country with no connections or safety net. We are ingenious, creative and entrepreneurial. We are scrappy and resilient; we have mastered the hustle.

Like generations of immigrants that have come to the US before us, we have an edge. I'll call it the Latino edge.

But as I mentioned before, many times we lack the mentorship, the inspiration, and business advice from successful Latino and Latina role models.

This is why I felt it was not only important but also *essential* that I start Logra Tu Dream and I write this book.

I want to do my part to help remove these barriers and inspire you to join the cause.

The Problem

Despite our edge, our superior work ethic, our creativity, and the tremendous progress of our people, many in our community are struggling to achieve their dreams. We are not maximizing our full potential, but once we do, I see a future in which Latinos & Latinas are a consistent presence at the top of every industry and every field in the US.

How are we struggling?

We are struggling to build wealth. According to Andres Gutierrez [2], a top Latino personal finance expert, more than fifty percent of Latinos have $1000 or less saved.

We are also struggling to maximize our potential. Only 15 percent of Latinos have a bachelor's degree compared to forty percent for whites and sixty percent for Asians/Islanders. Despite the great improvements over the last 20 years in Latino college enrollment, we are still well behind the white and Asian populations.

These groups are at the top of the success ladder in this country in large part because of their higher levels of education. Being behind in terms of education is setting us back and limiting our success. If more Latinos and Latinas improve their level of education, whether through school or self-education, their level of success would also increase.

We are still a minority at the top of corporate America. Even though we are creating businesses at a record pace, there are few Latino entrepreneurs succeeding in Silicon Valley and atop the highest growth industries in the nation like technology, robotics, etc.

We are struggling because we lack access to Latino and Latina role models who can mentor us and show us the way to success. Whether you are an immigrant or you were born in the US, it is very likely that your parents themselves didn't have a roadmap for success in this country, either.

They didn't have a roadmap because they either stayed back in their home countries or they were first-time immigrants who were trying to figure it out themselves.

We struggle because if we don't see examples of successful Latinos and Latinas achieving their dream, we believe it is not possible for us to achieve our dreams and we lose faith.

This is why it is critical to share these stories of successful Latinos and Latinas that show that "si se puede" (it is possible) and also reveal a system of success, illuminating a proven path to achieve your dreams.

The successful Latinos & Latinas you'll read about in this book have seen how other Latinos & Latinas have achieved their dreams. Because they have seen it is possible, they believe it is possible for them to make it and have also learned from others ahead of them how to achieve their success...

Chapter 4

BELIEVE THAT "SI SE PUEDE" (IT IS POSSIBLE)

"How can we continue to lift Latino success stories so that children see themselves in them?"

- *Maribel Duran, Chief of Staff White House Initiative on Educational Excellence for Hispanics*

43

Seeing is Believing

We come from hardworking families; our parents worked hard to give us a better future. But as I mentioned before, many times our parents had no roadmap to achieve success in this country because they were figuring it out for themselves.

This is why many times we have been at a loss at how to succeed in this country, and why successful Latino and Latina role models and their mentorship are so needed in our community.

It is hard to believe what we can't see. To believe in something, we need to see it first; this is why we tend to believe mostly in things that are visible to us.

One of the biggest barriers standing in the way of the dreams of millions of Latinos and Latinas in this country is the lack of belief that they can be successful.

Where does this mindset come from?

It comes from believing in what is around us. If we don't see successful people around us then we end up believing we can't be successful. We believe we can only be like the people we see around us.

One of my Logra Tu Dream listeners articulates this perfectly:

"Since listening to Logra Tu Dream and learning about the entrepreneurial stories of your guests, I have realized that Latinos really can be successful in the US. I personally don't know any Latinos who have successful professional careers and I think that is one reason why it has been difficult for me to begin my career."

When we are exposed to the stories of successful Latinos and Latinas as my listener was, we believe that it is possible. We believe because we realize that others like us with similar backgrounds have been able to overcome similar barriers we face.

We believe when we learn about how these role models overcame similar barriers we face, and how they went on to achieve their dreams. We realize there are common principles that together reveal a system of success that anyone can apply to their lives.

We realize that it doesn't matter where we come from, or whether we have money or social status. What matters is our mindset, our actions and our habits.

It is very possible to be successful, and your mind is the first that needs to totally embrace this fact. Because if your mind doesn't believe it; it will never happen.

If you believe it you can make it a reality

Thoughts turn into beliefs, beliefs turn into actions, actions turn into habits, and great habits transform your life for the positive.

The most successful people in the world and the top thinkers in the science and art of success, from Napoleon Hill to Tony Robbins, have written about this fact extensively.

The 50 successful Latinos and Latinas highlighted in this book show this same pattern. They all first believed they could accomplish their dreams and then they took massive action, which turned into the habits that led to their success.

Achieving your dream is within your reach. Only you can make the decision to change your life and adopt the mindset, actions and habits of success.

Lizza Monet Morales took control of her mindset at an early age. She has always believed she could accomplish anything she put her mind to through the example and inspiration of her mother and her grandmother.

"Our words form our thoughts, our thoughts form our actions, and our actions form our reality"

-*Lizza Monet Morales*, top Latina influencer, actress, TV host and content creator

Lizza, from humble beginnings, became the bumblebee flying high, achieving things most people thought would be impossible.

Her belief in her ability to achieve her dream drove her to get into Harvard University and Middlebury College, becoming the first in her family to go to college. She became a rising actress who has made a name for herself as a bilingual reporter, a brand ambassador, and a top Latina influencer.

Lizza has been on-air for Access Hollywood, Telemundo, EXTRA, Univision, Celebrity Justice, The Insider, and The TV-Guide Channel, among other media outlets. In addition, she has reported for Us Weekly and People Magazine and has been a columnist for Item Magazine. She's also served as a backstage correspondent at top award shows including the GRAMMYs, the Academy Awards. Latin Billboards and the Latin GRAMMYs. Acting wise, she was most recently featured in HBO's "Phil Spector" biopic.

Lizza shows us the power of believing in yourself, and she shows us that the dream is within reach to anyone who believes.

"You have to believe in yourself first before anybody else can"

- *Lizza Monet Morales*

But don't just take Lizza's word. If you have ever doubted yourself, continue reading and you'll know and believe that you can too, "si se puede" (it is possible):

- ✓ Deldelp Medina failed her way to success, becoming the founder and CEO of Avión Ventures and the co-founder of the Latino Startup Alliance.
- ✓ Hipatia Lopez successfully started Empanada Fork without any previous industry knowledge or experience. Inspired by her dream, she learned along the way and made Empanada Fork happen.
- ✓ At age 23, Fidel Vargas became the youngest elected mayor of a major city in the nation, without any name recognition and having never run for office before.
- ✓ Alex Torrenegra immigrated to the US, working at Starbucks and McDonald's to make ends meet. He went from surviving to becoming a successful hi-tech entrepreneur in only a few years. He made and lost $3 million in a startup, and then bounced back building Bunny, Inc. into a multimillion dollar business and a leader in its field.
- ✓ Andres Gutierrez, a Mexican immigrant, went from being deeply in debt to achieving financial freedom and working with Dave Ramsey to bring thousands of Hispanics financial peace.
- ✓ Marissa Fernandez, a Cubana born in New York City, worked her way to become the NFL's Hispanic marketing leader.
- ✓ Ambrocio Gonzalez arrived with nothing from Mexico; he toiled at all kinds of odd jobs before he found his success as a restaurant owner and as a renowned Latino Chef. He now owns five restaurants, has his own TV cooking show, and is the brand ambassador at Nuestro Queso, attracting a large following.

These Latinos and Latinas all believed that it was possible to achieve their dreams; they made a decision to take control and change their lives, which propelled them to overcome seemingly impossible barriers and achieve the highest levels of success.

So be inspired, because the only obstacle you face is created by you, and it is within your power to remove it.

Remember, it all starts with you realizing that what you want to accomplish with your life is possible...

Because you now know that many others just like you have overcome the biggest obstacles and accomplished their life missions.

So make the decision to believe, and take control of your destiny today. Like Jim Rohn said: *"Success is something you attract by the person you become."*

Action Steps

✓ Learn about how other Latinos and Latinas like you, many coming from more difficult circumstances than you, have achieved seemingly impossible dreams.
✓ Understand that your limiting beliefs are false.
✓ Realize that you can achieve what you put your heart and mind to as these inspiring people did.
✓ Take control of your mindset today.

Chapter 5
HAVE A BIG DREAM FOR YOUR LIFE

"If the dream is big enough, the odds don't matter"

- Robert Renteria, Author of From the Barrio to the Boardroom & Civic Leader

---

All of the successful people I interviewed had a big dream for their life. In the last chapter, we saw that if you believe in your dreams, you can make them reality. If you have no dreams or small dreams that is exactly what you will get, so dream BIG.

All of us have had some sort of limiting beliefs; these beliefs are the ones that rob us of our dreams. These beliefs are a product of what we see around us in our environment. In our community, limiting beliefs are very common, as most of us or our parents and grandparents have experienced the struggle of leaving their home country and trying to make it in the US.

You might have experienced lack of money, education or connections. You might be struggling with limiting beliefs that hold you back and unconsciously tell you that you can't make it, that you are not good enough, or that you don't have what it takes to achieve what you want in life.

The successful people I have interviewed and I am basing this book on have learned to eliminate these limiting beliefs from their mindset and instead have chosen to dream big.

"There are no limitations except for the ones we create for ourselves."

— Jackie Camacho, Author, Keynote Speaker and Entrepreneur

Jackie Camacho had big dreams for her life that she has embraced, visualized, believed, pursued, and turned into reality. She is only 32 years old and yet she is a seven-time author, a successful entrepreneur, and a sought-after speaker. Jackie is a constant presence in the national and local Chicago media.

She has achieved at 32 what few people achieve in a lifetime, but the most impressive thing about Jackie is that she is just getting started. She firmly believes that the sky is the limit, and if you meet her, you would agree with her, as I do. So how did Jackie Camacho, a young woman who immigrated to the US from Mexico at age 14, without speaking English and without any connections and little money, create such a level of success for herself so fast?

When Jackie emigrated at age 14, she came with a big American dream of becoming a successful entrepreneur and writing a book. From an early age, Jackie believed she could make her dream happen. She was inspired by the books she read as a kid, which taught her the way to make dreams a reality.

It was books like *Think and Grow Rich* from Napoleon Hill and the Greatest Mystery in the World from Og Mandino, among many others, that instilled dreams in her heart.

With this knowledge she visualized her dreams; she bought a Kindle device and imagined how one day she would download her own book from the device.

When she arrived in the US, she didn't speak English but she learned it in only two years, along with German. She excelled in school, studying marketing, and soon she was starting her own business, going to work on making her dream a reality.

But success didn't come easy. She was diagnosed with cancer at 21, and again at age 23. Facing her mortality at such an early age woke her up to the beauty of life, making her a very positive and grateful person.

She was able to beat cancer and thrive once she accepted what was happening to her. These difficult experiences strengthened her resolve to grab life by the horns and create the life of her dreams. She started to work towards her dream by getting a job at a restaurant group. She created a marketing initiative at her job, helping many small businesses with their marketing.

Then she decided to start her marketing business, and to her surprise many people that she had worked with contacted her, asking to become her clients. These people had been touched by Jackie's positive attitude, her personal touch, and by her ability to help people get results on their business.

Jackie wrote personal handwritten notes to people she met, making powerful first impressions that helped make Jackie memorable.

"You become what you think about"

- Earl Nightingale

Since 2006, when she started her business, it has grown organically, entirely by referrals from clients. Jackie hasn't had to go out to sell any business in more than eight years, and she has more business than she can handle. Her team has grown from one to fourteen people.

She lives by the saying, *"Yo voy a ser el bien sin saber a quien"* (I will do good without knowing to whom), helping many people along the way without expecting anything in return.

One day she was invited to share her story with a group, and soon after people were asking her to write a book about her story. This led her to write a book about her life in which she opened her heart, exposing her vulnerabilities which in turn forged incredible connections with many people who now follow her.

Jackie turned her dream into a strong belief in being able to make it a reality, which turned into daily actions and habits that got her closer to her dream every day. To turn thoughts into beliefs, beliefs into actions, and actions into habits, Jackie used daily visualization and affirmations.

She defined her dreams clearly around her passions of becoming a successful entrepreneur and author. This clarity proved to be very powerful as it guided her thoughts and daily actions. Jackie essentially programmed her mind to focus on making her dreams a reality at a conscious and unconscious level.

From Napoleon Hill, Tony Robbins, Jack Canfield and other top minds in the self-development arena, we know that Jackie's approach of systematically re-programming her mind to reach her dreams works. Countless successful people have used this technique to manifest what seemed to be the impossible in their lives.

We all have this ability to reprogram ourselves to be able to use our full potential in pursuit of our calling. If we don't deliberately program our mind, we will default to letting outside influences, which we don't control, program our minds.

This is why so many people wander aimlessly through life, chasing mirages and other peoples' dreams. No wonder so many feel disempowered and disenchanted with their lives.

This is why I have limited my exposure to negative influences like TV, other types of media, and negative people that just fill your mind with bad news and create anguish and other negative feelings. I can't tell you what a difference this has made in my life.

As Austin Netzley, the bestselling author of *Make Money, Live Wealthy,* who was a guest on the podcast, says: "I have cut out the news, TV and negative people." This completely changed his energy and helped him get rid of his limiting beliefs.

With this knowledge in hand, there is no reason why you should wait a second more to take control NOW and dream big. After all, dreaming big or small takes the same effort.

So why cut your dreams short? Go Big and never let anyone tell you that you can't achieve them. Many people who you'll read about in this book started in the worse possible situations, faced the toughest adversity, and yet they have accomplished their big dreams. And so can you.

Define your Dreams Clearly

Dreaming big is a great start, but to get on track to make your dream a reality you need to define with clarity what reality you want to create in your life. You need to see your vision of your future vividly in your mind, and you need to believe in your heart that you have already accomplished it.

You need to do this because being able to clearly visualize your dream and believe it in your heart will program your mind to go after and achieve your dreams, and convince your heart that you deserve your dream and that it is possible.

Deborah Deras, a life coach and speaker who was on the podcast, has experienced the incredible power of creating a vision board to bring dreams to life. Vision boards have helped her and many of her clients envision and bring their dreams to reality.

She did a vision board in which she envisioned herself speaking along with Marion Williamson, a well-known speaker and Oprah Winfrey's spiritual counselor. Some years later, her dream became a reality: they ended up speaking together at two conferences.

It is very easy to make your own vision board. All you need to do is write down what you want, the life you wish to create for yourself in all its dimensions: financial, family, relationships, your mission, spiritual, career, personal fulfillment, etc.

Here is my list of what I want to create in my life:

Family: I want to be able to spend half of my time with my kids and create wonderful, memorable moments with them. I want to be closer to my family in Mexico: my goal is to see my mom and sister at least three times a year and share priceless moments with them, too.

Relationships: I want to continue to grow my relationship with my wonderful girlfriend, Gina, and spend the rest of our lives together. I want to re-connect with old friends and make more time for new ones. I will continue surrounding myself with great people who will help me get what I want and who I can help do the same.

Mission: My mission is to help others achieve their dreams so I will continue working hard on this path to help you in your journey towards your dreams.

Spiritual: I am working towards getting more in touch with my soul and becoming more mindful of the wonderful experience I am having in this world. My aim is to be more present and more in tune to what really matters so I can craft the life that will bring me the most fulfillment and happiness.

Career: I want to continue to build a successful career as a brand builder, thought leader, podcaster, content creator, and now as an author and speaker. My dream is to help as many people as possible through my work.

Personal Fulfillment: I am on a quest to fully optimize and realize my full potential, happiness and my impact on this earth. I want to reach my limits in all these areas and live the fullest life possible for me.

Financial: My goal is to achieve financial independence by 2020. As you will see later in the book, financial independence means reaching a point in which you generate enough passive income to pay for your living expenses for the rest of your life. I want to be able to do whatever I want in my life without having to worry about money.

Once you have this very clear on paper, bring it to life with images that represent all these aspirations in a visual collage.

You can do it on a PowerPoint slide, or if you want a more sophisticated solution, there are a number of software tools you can use to make a wonderful and inspiring vision board.

Print it out and put it somewhere you can see it at various times during the day, every day. This could be in your office, bedroom, or home office. You should also have a digital version you can access through your phone or iPad.

Adopt a Morning Ritual

Most of the successful people I know and have come across have a morning ritual that puts them in a state of mind that is a critical component to their success. The ritual usually has a combination of meditation, exercise, affirmations, visualization, reading and journaling/gratitude exercise.

I adopted my daily morning ritual about five months ago, after I read *The Miracle Morning*, a book I highly recommend from Hal Elrod. Hal is a big proponent of meditation, as I am; I started meditating in January of this year (2015). Meditation has given me a deep sense of peace and mindfulness that I didn't have before. I find myself being more present, which has helped me enjoy the beautiful moments in life more.

It also has opened my mind to deeper insights about life, my work and my relationships. I believe that I have come up with better ideas because I meditate. Having better ideas has helped me become more successful in my work.

Meditation has reduced my stress levels, helping me face difficult situations with more calm and more effectiveness than before. I have become more aware, calmer and happier as a result.

I highly recommend you take up meditation. I was not surprised when I came across an article a few months ago about the large number of successful people who meditate. These people have found the tremendous benefits meditation can have on their lives and their careers.

It might seem daunting to start meditating if you have never done it before. I didn't know how to meditate when I started. What helped me tremendously was to lean on a couple of apps that teach how to meditate. My favorite apps are Headspace and Omvana; you can find them on iTunes or Google Play. Even after I learned to meditate, I continue to use them as they help me to meditate more deeply and effectively versus by myself.

My morning ritual has given me incredible peace and clarity of mind. It has also given me purpose and energy that has helped me thrive during a very busy period in my life: I have been juggling what amounts to about three jobs.

I am juggling my work at Nuestro Queso, where I started producing "Nuestra Cocina," a local TV show, all while continuing to refresh the brand and starting a new B2B initiative. I am doing my podcast, doing awesome speaking engagements, writing this book, and reading or listening to about three books a month. Most importantly, I spend as much time as I can with my precious kids and my girlfriend.

It has probably been the busiest period in my life, but it has been one of the most productive and rewarding, too. I don't think I could have done all this successfully without my morning ritual.

Affirmations & Visualization

"I am in the right place, at the right time, meeting the right people to use my skills, talents and abilities to be abundantly paid to do what I love"

- Deborah Deras, entrepreneur, life coach and speaker

Once you have your vision board, imagine that your dream has become a reality in all of its aspects. Write it down and break it up into specific goals you want to achieve: these are your affirmations.

Say them out loud every morning while looking at your vision board, imagining and feeling with all your heart that your dream life is a reality. Do this for 5-10 minutes every morning and you will see incredible results in your life.

Saying your daily affirmations consistently can change your life because over time affirmations re-program your mind at a subconscious level to lead a life that will achieve your dreams. Affirmations train your mind to believe that the life you want is already a reality so the minds goes out and directs you to make it so.

Affirmations will program you to seek the people, resources and opportunities that will enable you to create the life that you want. Affirmations will also put you in a state of mind that will enable you to maximize your potential, work hard and attract the right people and knowledge that you need in the life you envision for yourself.

Break your dream down into achievable short term goals

As I mentioned earlier, one of the best pieces of advice my late father gave to me when I asked him about his secret to success was to break down big goals into small, manageable, and achievable ones.

My father was a brilliant and very successful man, rising from humble beginnings to become a top computer industry executive in Mexico. And he knew what he was talking about: he once confided to me that he'd achieved everything he'd set out to achieve in his life.

I have successfully followed this advice many times in my life. It worked for me, and it will work for you, too. It works because it allows you to turn a huge, seemingly impossible dream into many small, achievable goals.

Take your affirmations and break them down into smaller manageable and achievable goals. Make these goals short-term and time-bound; write them down and give them a date for completion.

Share the goals and the dates by when you will complete them with your closest friends, family, and mastermind group, if you are in one. If you are not in a mastermind group yet, read on, as I will talk about them later.

Then focus relentlessly on achieving these short-term steps one by one, celebrating and moving on to the next as soon as you knock off each one.

Action Items

- ✓ Have a BIG dream for your life and define it very clearly.
- ✓ Write down and create a vision board with images that bring to life your BIG dream.
- ✓ Write down your affirmations: These affirmations should reflect in detail what you want to create in your life. Be specific about what you want to accomplish,

59

the abundance you want to create, the relationships you want to have, etc. Break the affirmations down into smaller manageable and achievable goals.

✓ Adopt a morning ritual you can do consistently in which you do a visualization exercise, say your affirmations out loud, meditate, exercise, write, and express gratitude. Imagine and feel your dreams becoming reality every single morning, and with time your unconscious mind will lead you to make your vision a reality in your life.

Chapter 6

BE GRATEFUL

"*I am very grateful to anybody that cares about what I have to say*"

- Gary Vaynerchuk , New York Time best-selling author, investor, and world changing entrepreneur

Being grateful for what you have puts you in a state of mind that creates attitudes that attract opportunities and the right people to your life. On the contrary, being angry that you don't have what you think you should puts you in a state of mind that repels opportunities and people.

Angelica Atondo is a former award-winning journalist. She was the Chicago TV station Univision anchor and has become an entrepreneur with one of the biggest social media audiences in Chicago.

Angelica has always been grateful to every person who helped her along the way. From an early age, she knew she could not succeed alone; she would need help from other people.

"I remember the name of every person that has given me a helping hand, and I am never going to forget them because I think part of the essence of every human being that wants to be successful in this life is to never forget who helped you along the way"

- Angelica Atondo, former Univision anchor, entrepreneur and author

By being grateful throughout her life, Angelica attracted many opportunities in her career. She started her career in a small, Arizona TV station after she was discovered while filming a TV ad in the station. Marco Flores and Ramon Pineda, the people who gave Angelica her first opportunity in TV, became her mentors. A few years later, Ramon told Angelica about the Chicago Univision anchor opportunity and urged her to do the casting call for it.

She did and got the job, and she thrived in the Chicago Univision anchor role. She grew her audience and invested time and effort in her development. She worked hard to build her personal brand and to gain the skills she would need to become a successful entrepreneur, speaker, and author when she left Univision some years later.

If Angelica had not being grateful to Ramon Pineda—who gave her the first opportunity in her TV career—he probably would not have become her mentor and brought her the Univision anchor opportunity which helped her career take off.

Judith Duval is a former finance executive and consultant who is now a certified leadership coach. She attended the Wharton School and Stanford Business School. Many people doubted that she could be successful at Wharton when she chose to major in finance, one of the toughest college majors in the country.

A teacher told her that she only got into Wharton because she was Latina. These people could have shot the confidence of many other people and discouraged them, but not Judith.

Instead, she pushed through and successfully completed her finance degree at Wharton. She went on to craft a very successful career and attend Stanford Business School. She is now grateful to those people that doubted her, as they fueled her to push through and achieve at the high level she always knew she was capable of.

Judith's mantra is "I'll find a way." She welcomes seemingly closed doors because she knows she can always find a way and figure it out.

So be grateful when you face adversity in your life. Adversity always brings a positive change that we might not recognize at the time we are going through it, but in the long term it always reveals itself.

Be grateful, not just because it is the right thing to do but also because it is smart to be grateful. Being grateful attracts great opportunities to your life like it did for Angelica. Being grateful attracts opportunities because most people are likely to want to help grateful people and run away from the ungrateful.

All of the 50 successful Latinos and Latinas featured in this book are incredibly grateful people. They make a point of expressing gratitude to people who help them, and they take time to reflect on what they are grateful for in their lives. It is clear that gratitude has been a very important factor in their success.

I have experienced firsthand the power of gratitude in my own life. It has been a liberating experience, to be grateful to be alive and in good health, and to be grateful for the people in my life: my precious kids, my loving girlfriend, my mother and sister, my good friends and all the fantastic people I have come across in my life.

Gratitude Exercise

I have made it a daily practice to write down in my journal what I am grateful for each day. Writing down what I am grateful for reminds me of how incredibly fortunate I am.

Realizing my good fortune puts me in a very positive state of mind which enables me to live my life with a positive energy that attracts great people and opportunities to my life.

This is a recent entry in my gratitude journal:

Today I am grateful for the opportunity to be able to make a living doing what I love, and to be able to have a podcast that reaches thousands of people, bringing inspiration and mentorship to their lives.

I am grateful to be writing the Logra Tu Dream book, which will help even more people by sharing the principles of success that I have learned through the podcast.

To express my gratitude to you for buying and reading my book, I would like to give you the Audiobook version 100% FREE! Go to: www.logratudream.com/freeaudiobook

Actions Steps

- Conduct the gratitude exercise:
  - ✓ To start your day with the feeling of gratitude, meditate every morning.
  - ✓ After your meditation, write down in a journal what you are grateful for that day.
  - ✓ Remind yourself what you are grateful for. This will put you in a very positive state of mind, which will enable you to live your life with a positive energy that attracts great people and opportunities to your life.

Chapter 7

EMBRACE THE ABUNDANCE MINDSET

"We have this little green monster called envidia (envy); we need to get past that because that is what is holding us back"

- Robert Renteria, author of *From the Barrio to the Boardroom* & *Civic Leader*

One of the biggest challenges holding back Latino success in America is the scarcity mindset. When I ask my guests about the biggest barriers we face in our community, this comes up again and again.

What is the scarcity mindset?

The scarcity mindset is one that sees fellow Latinos as our biggest source of competition instead of our biggest source of support. It is a destructive mindset that conceives a fixed pie instead of an expanding pie; it sees life as a zero sum game.

Unfortunately, many times the scarcity mindset is widespread in the Latino community. It is widespread because this mindset was so often the norm in the countries we came from.

I know this for a fact. Growing up in Mexico, I saw how corrupt governments with a scarcity mindset focused on taking from the people to enrich their own lives.

This pernicious influence created a widespread mentality of scarcity in which people believed that the only way to get ahead was to take down others who seemed to threaten their interests instead of collaborating with each other.

These beliefs crept into our community here in the US because they were passed down to us. Many times we didn't know any better; we had not experienced the fact that the more you help, the more you get back.

"We need to think more about collaboration, because that is something that doesn't happen that often in our community and unfortunately a lot of times Latinos are trying to take Latinos down"

- Tayde Aburto, President US Hispanic Chamber of E-commerce

The mindset of *"if I can't make it, you can't make it either"* is one of the biggest barriers to our progress. The consequences of the scarcity mindset are that sometimes we don't help each other as much as we should, and then we are not as successful as we can be.

Helping each other is critical to the success of any community because we don't succeed alone. One just needs to do some research on the success of the Indian and the Jewish community in America; you'll find that they actively help each other through strong support networks. They mentor each other, do business together and help each other. No wonder these are two of the most successful communities in America.

"We need to embrace the mentality of abundance within the Latino community and help each other to achieve higher levels of success"

- *Gianpaolo Pietri, Founder, Voto Hispano documentary*

We need to adopt a mindset of abundance because this is the mindset that works to achieve success. All of the successful people I have interviewed share this abundance mindset, as do the most successful people in the world, like Warren Buffett, Tony Robbins, Charlie Munger, etc. It is very clear that this is the mindset of success.

We need to realize that by helping each other we will all be more successful. This is the way we get ahead; we gain nothing by taking down fellow Latinos and Latinas.

Do you know any successful Latinos who don't collaborate with others in their communities?

Me, either.

Tayde Aburto is leading the charge to help small family Latino businesses thrive. He is doing this in part by teaching them to collaborate together to succeed together.

"We need to start collaborating more because there is a huge cake out there and we all can grab a piece of it"

- Tayde Aburto, President US Hispanic Chamber of E-commerce

He has been met with resistance from business owners with the scarcity mindset and from competing organizations that, instead of collaborating with his organizations, have tried to discredit them.

But he has been undaunted by this resistance and has been successful in spreading the mindset among many Latino family business owners.

One of the keys to the success of Fidel Vargas, CEO of the Hispanic Scholarship Fund, who has managed $1 billion in assets and who became mayor at 23 years of age, is embracing the abundance mindset.

Fidel has a practice of keeping a list of people he has come across in his life. He continually reaches out to them with opportunities he comes across, or articles or information that might be able to help them. Through reaching out and helping others, he has built a strong network of support, which has brought him great opportunities in life.

Fidel would not have adopted this practice if he were a scarcity thinker. He does this because he knows that the more he helps other succeed, the more successful he will become himself. He knows that life is not a zero sum game; he knows life is filled with abundance and there is enough to go around for everybody.

His incredible success is a testament that abundance thinking works, and abundance thinking is how successful Latinos and Latinas think.

Jesse Martinez and Deldelp Medina, the co-founders of the Latino Startup Alliance (LSA), are an excellent example of the power of embracing the abundance mindset in the Latino entrepreneurial community. They have set out to build a foundation that fosters an ecosystem to support Latino tech entrepreneurs.

They started the organization in 2011 when they found that there weren't any resources available to support Latino tech entrepreneurs in terms of networks, capital, mentorship, resources, etc.

The LSA provides awareness, access, and acceleration to Latino entrepreneurial ventures. They seek to connect them to sources of seed capital and to create the awareness of what it takes to become a successful tech entrepreneur. They have helped many Latino entrepreneurs by connecting them with the people and resources to access the capital and knowledge they need to get their startup off the ground.

Avion Ventures, a Latina-focused accelerator for mobile platforms led by Deldelp Medina, was born out of the LSA. Avion Ventures is helping accelerate a number of Latina startups. Both of these organizations are creating new Latino and Latina role models and are empowering Latino and Latina entrepreneurs to be successful. Both were born out of the abundance mindset.

As Latinos, we have extraordinary values that have been engrained by the example of our parents' sacrifice, hard work, and humility to give us a better life. The successful Latinos and Latinas I interviewed were inspired and influenced by how diligently their parents worked. As a

71

result, they have adopted the same values of hard work, sacrifice, and humility, always putting their families first.

These values, when coupled with applying the principles and mindset in this book, will propel you to a life filled with abundance. An abundance of happiness, fulfillment, health and wealth.

Let go of the scarcity mindset and embrace the abundance mindset. We have to empower each other and embrace each other. I started Logra Tu Dream to start a movement that inspires people in our community to help each other to achieve the American Dream. We lift ourselves by lifting each other up.

Action Steps

- ✓ Realize that the scarcity mindset leads to failure.
- ✓ Start helping others in your community. If you are an entrepreneur, help other entrepreneurs. If you have a job, help other people in your workplace.
- ✓ As you experience how having an abundance mindset brings you opportunities and success, spread it around, sharing your story to encourage others to do the same.

Chapter 8

INVEST IN YOURSELF TO BECOME A LEARNING MACHINE

"The minute we stop learning, we die"

- Lizza Monet Morales, top Latina influencer, actress, TV host and content creator

The best investment you can ever make is in yourself. The ability to learn, to adapt, and to master your domain are the most important skills you need to craft a life of success.

I don't know successful people who don't read. Reading nurtures your mind and your soul. Your mind and soul need high-quality food like your body. Great books are great mind and soul foods.

Imagine if you didn't feed your body appropriately. You would certainly get sick and could gain a lot of unhealthy weight. You could not function well, you would not have enough energy, and you would feel miserable.

If all you feed your mind and soul is low-quality food like TV, gossip magazines, and other worthless content, your mind and soul will not be able to function well, either. You will operate at a much lower level versus your potential. It will be all but impossible to make your dreams a reality.

So it is critical that you embrace the love of learning which will make you a lifelong reader. If you are reading this book, you are already on the right track.

Learning and reading about how successful people achieve their dreams has opened my mind to what really works in this world. I didn't know this when I started my journey, even though I had a great education from the Harvard Business School.

I didn't really have a sense of what it took to become successful. I was kind of lost and it has taken me years to figure out what really matters. Through avid reading about the most successful people in the world, and through interviewing the most successful Latinos and Latinas in

America, I now have a much better understanding of what works and what doesn't.

"The most powerful weapon is not a loaded gun but an educated mind"

- Robert Renteria, author of From the Barrio to the Boardroom & Civic Leader

This is very true, but to have an educated mind you must read, you must educate yourself, and you must learn throughout your lifetime. School learning comprises only a small fraction of what you need to learn. If you are serious about living a life that reflects the highest expression of yourself, you must continuously learn and enjoy the learning process.

You must develop a love for learning. Carol Dweck, the author of *Mindset,* identifies the growth mindset as the mindset of success. The growth mindset is one that recognizes that we can always improve by learning and practicing. The growth mindset drives us to a life of continuous learning and hard work because we believe we can always get better.

In contrast, the fixed mindset person thinks you're born with a certain ability that limits what you can accomplish. So fixed mindset people don't invest in lifelong learning; they avoid the big challenges for fear of failure. Fixed mindset people don't change the world, growth mindset people do.

Carol Dweck clearly shows that ability is not fixed; it improves with practice and learning. This is why you need to become a learning machine.

But you can't be a learning machine if you don't love knowledge so you must come to love learning. This, my friends, is the secret of learning.

Mariana Ferrari, founder of ComoCambiarLaVida.com, embraced the growth mindset and became a learning machine after deciding to leave the corporate world. She was a single mother of two kids who relied on her. Without a job, she needed to find a way to support them, and she started by discovering herself.

The turning point was when she understood that she could change herself. She looked for answers in books, becoming a learning machine. She studied Tony Robbins, Neurolinguistic programming, and many other coaching courses she could get her hands on.

She got rid of the limiting beliefs that had tied her down before. No longer did she believe she could not reinvent herself, or that there wasn't enough for everybody to go around. Many of these beliefs she had learned from her parents and her environment.

By discovering herself, she found her calling in life, which was to help others change their lives for the better. She identified what made her eyes shine and what made her unique. Since then, she has succeeded in helping many people reinvent themselves and live more fulfilling, successful lives.

In the process, Mariana has built a thriving business, becoming a top success coach and motivator in the Latino community, having been featured on Univision's national TV morning show, *"Despierta America."*

The importance of learning *how* to think, not what to think

The most important skill to succeed in the future is the ability to adapt and create. We are constantly influenced to consume more products and services. But to thrive we need to become creators, not consumers. And to become creators, we need to learn to adapt.

In school we are taught that the kids who score better on the tests are the smarter ones, and that they are more likely to succeed. So we are programmed to memorize facts and score well on tests, but we don't learn how to *learn*. In school, they teach kids what to think instead of teaching them how to think

We don't learn that we need to question things and think like creators. Instead, kids are taught to think like robots that should not question conventional wisdom.

"Never stop learning"

-Sonia Farace, entrepreneur

To learn how to adapt and to become a creator, you need to become a learning machine. To become a learning machine, you need to read every good book you can find on topics that you deeply care about and are critical to a life of happiness, wealth and health.

Aside from reading nowadays, you can access education online, where you can learn almost anything for little or no money. You can learn about almost anything you are interested in on YouTube, podcasts, online courses, and audio books. There is no excuse for not learning, as anyone can access the knowledge they need to develop themselves easily, instantly, and at little to no cost.

Udemy, Coursera or iTunes University are just some of the top online education platforms where you can find courses on every conceivable topic from the world's top experts and universities. These MOOCs (Massive Open Online Courses) are offered for free or for very low costs.

Become an autodidact and it will pay off handsomely. Put what you learn into practice until you master what you are learning.

Like Warren Buffett says, *"You have to learn to earn."*

Charlie Munger, who is a billionaire himself and Warren Buffett's partner, advises us to go to bed a little wiser every day.

To do this, take up the habit of reading for at least 30 minutes every single day in the morning or before going to bed.

Here is a list of books that I have read and highly recommend you read, too, as I have found them immensely valuable and inspiring. They have helped me in my journey to get closer to my dream and I have no doubt they will help you, as well:

- Zero to One, Peter Thiel
- The E-Myth Revisited, Michael Gerber
- Essentialism, Greg Mckeown
- The Alchemist, Paulo Coelho
- Meditations, Marcus Aurelius
- The ONE Thing, Gary Keller
- Poor Charlie's Almanac, Charlie Munger
- Choose Yourself, James Altucher
- The Art of Being Unmistakable, Srinvas Rao
- The Richest Man in Babylon, George S. Clason

- Think and Grow Rich, Napoleon Hill
- Man's Search for Meaning, Victor Frankl
- Total Recall, Arnold Schwarzenegger
- Mindset, Carol Dweck
- The Selfish Gene, Richard Dawkins
- The Miracle Morning, Hal Elrod
- Bold, Peter Diamandis
- The Millionaire Next Door, Thomas J. Stanley
- Launch, Jeff Walker
- Give and Take, Adam Grant
- Money Master the Game, Tony Robbins
- Smartcuts, Shane Snow
- The 4-Hour work week, Tim Ferris
- The Total Money Makeover, Dave Ramsey
- Rich Dad, Poor Dad, Robert Kyosaki
- How to Win Friends and Influence People, Dale Carnegie
- Managing Oneself, Peter Drucker
- The Compound Effect, Darren Hardy
- Lessons of History, Will and Ariel Durant
- Crush it , Gary Vaynerchuk
- Jab, Jab, Jab, Right Hook, Gary Vaynerchuk
- Outliers, Malcolm Gladwell
- The Millionaire Messenger, Brendon Bruchard
- Mastery, Robert Greene
- The Success Principles, Jack Canfield

Feeding your spirit

Investing in yourself shouldn't be just about your mind. You need to feed your spirit, too; otherwise you will burn out. Like the body and the mind, the spirit also needs nourishment. To feed your spirit focus on having experiences that you know will fill your soul.

For me, sharing memorable moments with my kids, family and friends, listening to beautiful music, reading a book that touches me at a deep level, and helping others get closer to their dreams are all things that fill my soul.

The more I feed my soul, the more energy and passion I have for my life, my work, my health and my relationships. It has definitely paid off handsomely to feed my spirit with premium fuel.

So look for experiences that fill you with deep emotion as they will feed your spirit.

College and Graduate School

Even though school learning is just the tip of your learning iceberg, it can provide a strong foundation to establish a pattern of lifelong learning.

If you are reading this, it is very likely that your parents sacrificed a lot to provide you the best education possible, or you believed in yourself enough to know that you needed a good strong education.

Many of you might have been the first in your family to go to college or graduate school. Achieving this higher level of education in itself is a big accomplishment. I know it was for me when I was able to graduate from the Harvard Business School. My parents had gone to college, but nobody in my family had emigrated and gone to graduate school, much less one like Harvard.

It was surreal to me; I could not believe it was happening to me. Getting an education in this country was my ticket to the dance as it allowed me to ultimately stay in the US and build a life here.

We all want the very best education for ourselves and our children. After all the cumulative earnings of college graduates net of loan repayment for tuition and fees exceed that of high school graduates[3]. But the costs of college and graduate school have skyrocketed.

The average student loan debt has climbed to $29.4K and is equivalent to roughly 60 percent of graduates' annual income. The graph below shows how debt has skyrocketed over the last 10 years, while the median income of individuals with a bachelor's degree has plummeted.

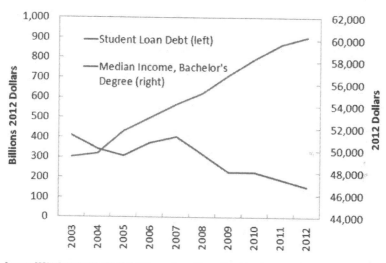

Sources: FRBNY Consumer Credit Panel, US Census Bureau Current Population Survey, BLS Consumer Price Index

Many students are taking on even bigger debt burdens that take years to pay off. Many times, the debt forces them to take jobs they might not want and it slows down their ability to build wealth as they are unable to save enough money.

The worst situations are when these college and graduate school graduates study degrees in fields that don't pay much. So they graduate and find themselves in low paying jobs with big debt burdens. Sometimes they take jobs in other fields unrelated to their field of study and struggle to pay their bills; many times, these are jobs that don't require much education.

The reality is that because of the high costs of college and graduate school, and because not all degrees have a good return on investment, college education sometimes does not pay off for many graduates.

So what gives? There has to be a better way...

How should we as parents guide our children when it is time for college so that they have a great start with the prospect of a good income and no debt?

Find ways to pay for college without student loans

On episode 32 of the Logra Tu Dream podcast, I interviewed Celest Horton, the founder of *"How to Pay for College HQ."*

Celest teaches people how to pay for college without student loans. Back before the Internet, she was able to search and secure enough scholarships to fully fund her education and all expenses.

She now helps families with strategies to get financial aid, merit aid and private scholarships for their kids. Celest has realized that if you are a good student, or a parent of a good student, and you put in the time and effort in learning how to tap the available scholarships and aid out there, you can fund a college education without student loans.

The problem is, most people don't even know about all the scholarships and aid that exists, and if they know, they don't know how to get it. This is why if you are a college student or a parent of a future college student you, need to inform

82

yourself and become an expert in how to pay for college without student loans as soon as middle school. Celest breaks down the three key sources of non-debt college funding:

1. **Financial Aid:** These are funds provided by the government, which are based on financial need. There are ways to get this aid even if you think you don't qualify.

2. **Merit Aid:** This is aid from universities to attract special students. It is based on student accomplishment, so it is important to identify early on where your kid can shine and encourage and help him to do so. Most private schools offer an incredible amount of money in merit aid that students don't have to pay back.

3. **Private Scholarships:** You need to apply for these scholarships, and it takes time and work. So it is important to find out about them early on. According to Celest, you have 1 in 10 odds to land a scholarship, so you need to apply to a lot of them so you can secure scholarship money.

Celest has also uncovered a fantastic opportunity in taking the PSAT test to have a shot at scholarship money. Not a lot of people know that this test, which is taken during the junior year in high school, also doubles as a National Merit Scholarship qualifying test. If you do very well on this test, you can get a full ride for college, so it pays to plan and prepare as much as you can for it.

Besides the usual academics and sports based scholarships there are also scholarships based on art, community service and other types of merit. So even if you are not at the top of your class, you still have a shot at getting scholarship money to finance your studies in the US. You just need to do your homework to educate yourself about all the different sources of non-debt financial aid to finance your education or your children's.

Celest provides a fantastic service helping people learn how to pay for college without getting into debt; I highly recommend you check her out at: www.howtopayforcollegehq.com

Cristian Arcega is a brilliant, former Latino high school student who was part of the team that won a robotics competition versus MIT, which in turn inspired the Spare Parts movie with George Lopez.

He received a full college scholarship but due to being undocumented, his scholarship was revoked a year into his engineering degree because of immigration legislation in Arizona.

He was no longer considered an in-state student and his tuition tripled. He has struggled to remain in school since. Ten years later, he still has not had the funds to attend college full time and complete his dream to become an electrical engineer.

So Cristian started a crowd-funding campaign to fund his education on www.Crowdisimo.com, and he raised $48K, 27 percent of the $178K he needs to pay for his degree. Cristian's case shows the irony of the challenges some Latinos and Latinas face in this country.

Despite Cristian's brilliance and notoriety, he has not been able to get a college education. But in the process, he has figured out an alternative way to pay for his degree. There is a lot to be learned from Cristian's struggle and his out-of-the-box thinking when it comes to finding ways to fund a college education without going into debt.

Crowd-sourcing isn't for everyone, but it is a good example of finding sources of non-traditional financial support.

Avoid getting in debt for a degree with a terrible ROI

All types of degrees cost a lot of money. Yet as I mentioned, not every degree has a good return on your investment, especially if you go into debt to fund it.

I don't advocate choosing your degree based on how much money you think you can make with it, but I strongly recommend that you try to avoid getting in debt for any degree, especially if it has low income potential.

The first step is to figure out your income potential after you graduate with your chosen degree and the other career options it will open. There are many online sources that help you figure out the income potential for different career paths. If you want to become an entrepreneur then you should do your homework and understand how much your degree will help you to become successful in your ventures.

Not every high school graduate wants to become an engineer or a computer scientist, which are college degrees that have higher ROIs. So what do you do if you or your child wants to study for a degree where the income potential is very low?

Some experts advise to either pay for it without debt, as I just laid out, or to find alternative ways to gain this knowledge that doesn't involve going into debt to get an expensive degree that the market does not value.

Peter Thiel, a billionaire who was one of the co-founders of PayPal and best-selling author of *Zero To One*, has an even

85

more controversial stance on college. He grants $100K fellowships to young people who undertake entrepreneurial projects in lieu of going to college:

> "Knowledge may be priceless, but a higher education is clearly not. University administrators keep hiking tuition, the wages of graduates keep falling, and a whole generation of Americans is struggling under the crushing burden of debt as they postpone their dreams for a tomorrow that may never come.
>
> There's a system that's telling people that you do certain things and you'll be fine. We need to be asking way tougher questions about that. I don't think there's anything wrong with the liberal arts. I think there is a problem with amassing $100,000 of student loans in something where you can't get a really well-paying job out of it on the other end."

So, what's the alternative?

Thiel's answer to this question is that students need to start figuring it out on their own.

This might be controversial to many, but there is a case to be made for figuring it out on your own, taking the autodidact road if a chosen career will not be worth the cost of getting a college degree in that field.

Fortunately, there are countless options to get a free or affordable education online today. If this applies to you, I encourage you to learn through mentorship, reading, and on the job training. Some of the MOOCs (Massive Open Online Courses) sites now offer certificates for completed classes that cost a little money but offer a way to document the attainment of online education.

The market will reward the value you are able to create, and these sources offer inexpensive ways to learn what you need to go into fields that will not reward an expensive degree.

Choose full rides over prestigious schools that require student debt to attend

Recently I ran across an article about Ronald Nelson, a new college student who was accepted to all the Ivy Leagues and Stanford, but elected to go to the University of Alabama because he was offered a full ride and got into its selective honors program.

He turned down the opportunity to go to Harvard, Stanford and all of the other Ivy League schools because he received only partial tuition from these universities, and would have had to go into debt to attend.

It does not matter where you get your college degree. What matters is how much you learn and how well you apply what you learn when you go out in the world.

Frank Bruni, a New York Times columnist, is the author of the book *Where You Go Is Not Who You'll Be*. In his book, he shows plenty of examples and offers lengthy stories of Americans of all ages and from all walks of life who have found success without degrees from brand-name universities.

Bruni points out that, among the American-born chief executives of the top 100 companies in the Fortune 500, just about 30 percent went to an Ivy League school or equally selective college. Which means that 70 percent of Fortune 500 CEOs did not attend an Ivy League school, yet did pretty well.

For Ronald Nelson, attending an Ivy Leagues school instead of a less prestigious, albeit good school like the University of Alabama, will not make much difference in terms of income and career potential over the long term. In his own words:

"I talked to my parents, and they told me, 'It won't be easy, but we could make this happen.' I wasn't sure if I wanted them to spend that money now or wait until later, when I'll be using it for a graduate degree."

His father, Roland Sr., elaborated on his son's decision. "*I think it would have been possible, given some sacrifice," he said.* "With people being in debt for years and years, it wasn't a burden that Ronald wanted to take on and it wasn't a burden that we wanted to deal with for a number of years after undergraduate."

Ronald made the right decision. He will get a great education for free with NO debt. That is what I call a great start!

Action Items

- ✓ Identify and write down what areas you need to develop in and what you need to learn about to accomplish this.

- ✓ Turn off the TV. I have almost eliminated TV-watching from my life and it has given me back so much time that I now use to pursue my dreams writing my book, doing my podcast, and reading.

- ✓ Read or listen to a book every day for at least 30 minutes. Check out my recommended books list above, which I have carefully curated by learning from the most successful people in our community and in the world.

✓ I highly recommend you subscribe to www.logratudream.com/audible. It is a fantastic source of knowledge. You can find almost every book in audio format there. I love it because I can listen to audible on my commutes or when I exercise, which allows me to get healthy and learn at the same time. I refuse to waste any time in my life anymore.

✓ Listen to podcasts on topics you want to learn from. There are thousands of terrific podcasts on every topic you can imagine, on iTunes and on Stitcher if you have an Android device. I became addicted to learning after I started listening to podcasts. I love to learn through podcasts because I learn through stories, which make what I learn so much more interesting and engaging.

✓ Find online courses about the topics that you care about; there are many free courses at udemy.com, great videos on every topic on YouTube.com, and a wealth of paid courses you can find online.

✓ Feed your spirit with the moments and experiences that fill the soul. Capture moments of happiness as much as you can, as these moments will provide fuel to keep you motivated along the way.

✓ If you are a student or a parent of a student planning to go to college, learn how to pay for college without debt. Avoid going into debt for a degree the market will not reward, and when in doubt, choose full rides over prestigious schools if that means going into debt.

The most important thing you must keep in mind is that to be able to get into the habit of learning every day, you must come to enjoy learning. So make it fun by reading and learning about what makes your heart sing and by learning in fun ways. In my case, I love learning by listening to podcasts and audio books; for you, it might be You Tube videos, online MOOC classes, or free courses at your local library.

As long as you are enjoying the learning process, it doesn't matter how you learn; what matter is that you learn something every day. If you do this, you will be amazed at how you'll transform your mind and your life as you apply what you learn towards achieving your dream.

Chapter 9
TAKE MASSIVE ACTION

"Make action our domain"

-Jose Huitron, Founder, Crowdisimo and Hub 81 venture design agency

Having a big dream, the right mindset and becoming a learning machine are critical to success, but if you don't take massive action your dream will not become a reality. To make your dream a reality, you need to transform your thoughts into actions and your actions into habits.

Sometimes transforming your dreams into actions is hard because it can be hard to figure out what actions to take.

As I mentioned before, breaking down your goals into smaller goals is how you can make a huge dream possible. But you still need to take massive action to accomplish those smaller goals. All your great intentions, you vision board and your affirmations will not do any good if you don't take action.

You'll need to take action even if you are afraid and have never done what you are about to do. You need to take action even if you have no skills or experience, and feel totally unprepared and unworthy of your aspirations.

Action is critical because it gets you in the stream. You can't swim towards your next destination if you are standing outside the water. You need to get in the water and start swimming; very soon you'll be in the water with other people and with the resources you need to get ahead.

"Be patient and see it through"

- *Hipatia Lopez, Founder and CEO Empanada Fork*

Hipatia Lopez worked in public accounting; she had never been an entrepreneur and knew nothing about how to run a business, and yet she went on to start Empanada Fork.

Hipatia had an idea of how to make empanadas much faster and with greater ease in comparison to how they had been made for decades. After the Empanada Fork idea came to her at a family gathering, she knew this was the business she should pursue.

But she was afraid of losing her hard-earned money by investing in the idea because she didn't know how to go about starting a business. However, when she realized that her family fully supported her and encouraged her to go forward, she decided to take action.

First, she contacted lawyers to determine how to get a patent for her idea; she researched everything about patenting her idea. She learned about the high costs of patents, but still decided to go forward and file for a design patent to protect her idea.

She handed her rudimentary drawing to her lawyer, who then asked a family member who was an architect to do the actual design. She waited for the patent approval before making prototypes and starting to go out and sell the product.

She knew intuitively that the product would be a hit. Once she received the patent, she went to Google to find manufacturers. She found a manufacturer in the US but the prototype failed. She was very disappointed and almost gave up at that point.

Hipatia then decided to get the Empanada Fork manufactured in China because she learned that she would be able to manufacture the Empanada Fork with high quality and at lower costs there.

She took the new and improved prototype to Latino restaurants to get feedback. Restaurants loved the product, which gave her the validation she needed to prove that her business had potential.

She started to try to sell her product to a number of big retailers like Wal-Mart and Bed, Bath and Beyond, but she was met with resistance from them. They doubted her ability as a small company to come through with large orders.

She was not deterred, and continued to approach local store managers with the product until they came around. Hipatia had made progress, but she knew she needed to hustle more to make her business a success.

So she took action again, joining and winning a QVC inventors contest. This was the big break she needed, which led to a lot of media attention. Realizing that big box stores were tough to penetrate, she decided instead to focus on online stores and was met with good success.

Because she took action through trial and error, Hipatia was able to get her product patented and manufactured, and then found the right channels to sell the product. In the process, her actions drew the attention of the media and her community, which helped raise awareness about her product. This in turn opened many retailer and distributor doors.

Hipatia continues to grow her business by expanding her network, which brings her even more opportunities. One of these opportunities was to do cross promotions with Goya, the Latino food giant, which brought her even more exposure.

Before she started, Hipatia didn't know the first thing about how to turn her idea for a business into a reality. But by taking action, she got in the stream that led her to the people, the knowledge and the opportunities that have

94

helped make Empanada Fork a successful, growing business with tremendous potential.

Simply put, Hipatia got in the game. Her first step created forward momentum, which then led to the next step, and so on. She did not let the setbacks stop her, when her first prototypes didn't work she got a better manufacturer. When big box retailers turned her down she kept moving forward, successfully shifting her focus to online stores.

Each win along the way led to the next opportunity; her success compounded one step at a time until she made her business successful. This would not have happened if she had not taken the first step.

Action creates forward momentum that if not interrupted can only take you in the direction of your dreams. In life, as in physics, movement is the spark that starts the trajectory of a moving body towards its destination. So take action and get moving!

"It doesn't take a fancy education, it just takes hard work"

- Toby Salgado, entrepreneur and multi-millionaire

Toby Salgado knows that there is no easy street or magic pill that can make you successful. He has worked very hard for everything he has in life.

As an entrepreneur in college, he started a painting company from scratch. In the space of two years, he was making $50K a year with his venture while still attending school. He had no previous experience or clients: he just made it happen by knocking on a lot of doors, offering to paint people's houses, and then doing a great job painting those houses.

Encouraged by his initial venture, Toby was determined to find even more business opportunities he could capitalize on. He went straight to the top, calling the CEO of a big home building company and asking him about the main issues he was dealing with. In speaking with him, Toby realized there was an opportunity to offer erosion control services to homebuilders. So he went right back to the CEO and offered erosion control services.

He didn't have experience, a business license, employees or equipment, etc. But he did his research on erosion control by reading a book and when he met with the homebuilder, he realized he knew more than they did.

At the end of the meeting, he had a contract for $46K for a project. He went to Home Depot; got the equipment he needed, and found a few guys off the corner to help him with the project. He made $26K in a week.

He leveraged the fact that he had worked with this prominent homebuilder to call on other homebuilders. His initial job gave him instant credibility and helped him get more business. He made $350K in the first year, $600K in the second year and $986K by the fourth year. With no previous experience, equipment or even employees, he made almost $1 million in only four years by taking massive action.

Then the homebuilding business dried up and Toby realized it was time to move on to the next opportunity. Taking the same approach as before, he took action again.

At this time, the market had crashed and banks were not lending money. He identified an opportunity to lend money to a company that needed operating capital for the next six months. The company had $33 million in secured real estate assets so there was really no risk.

He raised $2 million from friends and family and tripled his money in a few months. Next, he found a deal in which he bought a property for $3.2 million that was in default and sold it back to the same builder for $9 million only three years later.

Toby became a multimillionaire at the age of 35. He has a tremendous ability to spot and capitalize on opportunities. But most importantly, he takes action when he spots these opportunities and works harder than most people.

Hustlear (Hustling)

"It is really pretty simple, you just need to hustle"

- Gianpaolo Pietri, Founder "El Voto Hispano" documentary

To hustle is to be continuously getting into the stream of opportunities by working hard to meet the right people and create opportunity for yourself. To hustle is to not be complacent; it is to always be hungry, and to always be trying to improve yourself.

Gianpaolo Pietri is the founder of *El Voto Hispano* a feature documentary about the power and influence of Latino voters in US elections. The project is being produced by Eva Longoria and recently became the most funded Latino-led project on Kickstarter.

Gianpaolo believes that you must lose your fear to reach out to influential people who can help you. He cold-called, sent emails, and when they said no, he tried again and again.

He managed to get Eva Longoria as a producer on the project by hustling like his life depended on it. He showed the project to a friend, who showed it to an actor who knew Eva. The actor fell in love with the project and brought it to Eva. The topic was hot in the media at the time and Eva loved the project and the Kickstarter video. She jumped in and became the producer of the project.

With Eva on board now, they had social proof and all types of media picked up the story. *El Voto Hispano* had become newsworthy and it was firing on all cylinders. The Kickstarter campaign was very successful, raising $100K, which was just what Gianpaolo needed to go forward with the documentary.

Gianpaolo and his team have been filming the documentary ever since. They will film through 2016 to cover the presidential election, interviewing top politicians and covering the whole election process. They will release the full documentary after the 2016 election. They are accomplishing something truly important, raising awareness about the growing power and political influence of Latinos in America.

This dream is becoming a reality because of Gianpaolo's hustle. Without the hustle, it would still be just a dream.

Making your dream a reality is not easy, and it does not come overnight. You may fail more than once in your journey to success, but if you keep hustling you will eventually achieve your dream. Your success will be a measure of how bad you want it and how hard you work for it:

"Failures are not failures; they are opportunities to continue growing."

- Mauricio Simbeck, CEO Milagros de Mexico

Our community is blessed with ingenuity and hustle; it is part of who we are as a people, from the immigrant hustle of millions who have come to this country with nothing to start a new life, to the hustle of their children, who work incredibly hard to get ahead in this country.

Hustle is in the Latino DNA; we are hard-workers by nature so if you are hustling but not getting closer to your dream every day, then you need to work on your mindset.

If you have the right mindset as I discussed in the previous chapters and you have hustle, you have what it takes to be incredibly successful. So capitalize on your edge and hustle!

Action Steps

- ✓ Lose the fear and take the first step
- ✓ Get in the stream of people, knowledge and opportunities that will lead you to success in your field
- ✓ Continuously take action to create the next opportunity
- ✓ Compound one win on top of the previous one to create momentum
- ✓ Aggressively pursue the opportunities that feel right for you
- ✓ Work HARDER than anybody else
- ✓ Hustle like your life depended on it

Chapter 10

GET MENTORED

"There isn't someone in my immediate circle to whom I can go to for career advice, so again Logra Tu Dream has been helpful to me and this is why I am reaching out to you."

- Logra Tu Dream podcast listener

There is a lack of mentorship in the Latino community

"If you want to be successful, find someone who has achieved the results you want and copy what they do and you'll achieve the same results."

- Tony Robbins

I have learned that the main barrier to achieving the American Dream in the Latino community is the lack of Latino & Latina mentors and the lack of mentorship. This is the main reason I started my Logra Tu Dream podcast and why I am writing this book. I have seen and experienced this problem firsthand.

There is a lack of Latino/Latina mentors and role models who can show others the path to success because mentorship is not something that is ingrained in our culture. Aside from our parents and extended families, most young Latinos and Latinas don't have access to mentors who can guide them. This is a tragedy because the potential of millions is not being maximized.

We know that mentorship is a crucial ingredient to achieving at the highest levels. As you are learning in this book, nobody succeeds by themselves without some sort of guidance from more successful people than themselves.

Having access to relatable role models that show it is possible to achieve the highest levels of success is critical to our community. It is critical because our young people need to be able to see themselves in Latinos & Latinas who have achieved at the highest levels.

Our struggle is unique and our people need to know and see that others just like them can make it, because then they'll know that they can make it themselves.

To top it off, many times we don't ask for help. We don't know who to ask or how to ask. We are just not taught to ask for help as we grow up.

Deldelp Medina, the founder of Avion Ventures and co-founder of The Latino Startup Alliance, puts it best:

"The other big mistake I have made is not knowing who to listen to and not knowing when to ask for help. My parents raised me in a very independent way and I am not very good at asking for help."

For all these reasons, there is a huge lack of mentorship in the Latino community. This is one of the biggest factors holding us back from fulfilling our maximum potential and becoming as successful as we can be.

Why even the most successful people in the world have a mentor

"You learn from mistakes but they don't have to be yours"

- Warren Buffett, CEO Berkshire Hathaway and second richest man in the world

103

Even the most successful people in the world have mentors. They have mentors because they have realized that being able to learn through somebody else's experience can save them years of hard knocks and failure.

All the successful people I have interviewed have had mentors at different points in their lives. Having a mentor accelerated their careers.

Alex Torrenegra, the founder of Bunny Inc. and a very successful entrepreneur, started his journey working at Starbucks and McDonald's when he first immigrated to the US.

Alex is a born entrepreneur. He made $3 million with the first venture he started but lost it all in his next venture. He had not reached out to mentors, as he was afraid to ask for help, and he paid dearly for not getting mentored.

For the next venture, which became Bunny Inc., the leading voiceover marketplace in the world, he decided to get mentored to avoid the mistakes he had made in the past.

How mentorship helped Alex Torrenegra achieve his dreams

Alex first identified people who he thought could help him achieve success in his venture. These were successful people, many of them years ahead of Alex in terms of life experience and careers, who were in a position to help him by sharing what they had already learned about what worked and what didn't.

Then he reached out to these people, sometimes via Twitter, and asked them to meet him for coffee to get their feedback on his business. Most of them did not respond but the ones who did were worth all the time and effort he put into it. He asked these mentors to introduce him to other people so that he could grow his mentor base.

Through this approach, Alex was able to get mentored by Reid Hoffman, the founder of LinkedIn, who gave Alex a half hour of his valuable time to offer advice that helped shaped Bunny, Inc. He was also mentored by a slew of investors, executives and entrepreneurs who advised him in all aspects of his business.

Through this mentorship, he learned that he should focus on one startup at a time. He learned how to market, how to build his team, and how to finance his startup, among countless other important lessons.

He found that his mentors positively influenced all the important decisions in his startup, Bunny, Inc. The mentoring he received directly impacted his venture and helped him make Bunny Inc. the leading marketplace for voiceover talent in the world.

Alex applied what he learned from his mentors. This was critical in order for them to take him seriously and to want to continue to help him. Having access to these super successful people elevated his game dramatically. Alex is very grateful for all the help he received and is now giving back. He has become an advocate for other entrepreneurs.

He founded Torrenegra Labs, an incubator named one of the top immigrant startups by Forbes. He also founded BogoTech, BogoDev, and HubBog, the three largest communities of web entrepreneurs, software developers, and technologists in Colombia.

"You ask for help not because you are weak but because you need to remain strong"

- Robert Renteria, Author From the Barrio to the Boardroom & Civic Leader

When I came to this country 18 years ago, I didn't know what a mentor was. I failed at my start up right after business school and I learned the hard way that if I wanted to be successful, I needed a mentor.

During this experience, I didn't have a mentor who could have helped me avoid many of the mistakes I made. I didn't have a mentor because at the time I didn't really understand the importance of having one.

I didn't know that mentors are key to success. I didn't know that having a mentor can be the closest thing to having the experience of the most successful people in your field but without actually having to go through the pain of acquiring it through costly trial and error.

I didn't know because nobody guided me and shared this knowledge with me. I didn't seek mentorship because, simply put, I didn't know what I didn't know. I was also scared to ask for help because I didn't want to look dumb.

When in fact I was dumb because I didn't ask for help...

I went through the pain of failing with my startup; I experienced considerable financial pain, and my young marriage suffered because of it. I worked incredibly hard but I didn't do a crucial thing that could have saved me a lot of that pain. I didn't validate the idea first with minimal investment. If I had, I would have learned that the idea was too early for its time and I would have pivoted and either changed the idea or focused on something else.

Making big mistakes that could be avoided by having a good mentor can be very painful and costly, and can set you back in your career and life. If you could save years of your life getting where you want to be and avoid costly mistakes that can set you back significantly, why would you not do it? Right?

If you agree with me, as I think most of you reading will, then you just agreed to get mentored...

How to get a mentor

First, you need to identify people who have accomplished what you would like to accomplish, and who you can see yourself becoming in the future. Shoot for the top: you'd be surprised by how open many of the top people in their fields are to mentoring younger people with a lot of hustle and a will to succeed. They are willing to help because most successful people are generous and want to give back, and because they see themselves in these hungry mentees.

One day I was walking the streets of Chicago when I saw Gary Vaynerchuk heading towards me while he crossed the street. I stopped him and asked him to be a guest on the podcast and he agreed.

Gary V. is a New York Times bestselling author, a multimillionaire entrepreneur, and a celebrity in the media and entrepreneurial worlds. But yet he took the time out of his incredibly busy life to be a guest on my podcast. During our interview, I asked him why he had agreed to come on.

He said he agreed to be on the show because I showed great hustle by asking him on the street and because, despite his great success, he continues to hustle harder than ever to reach more people. So for him, being on my podcast gave him an opportunity to reach people he wouldn't have reached otherwise.

So don't be afraid to shoot high; you might be pleasantly surprised.

The Bring Value Approach

Once you have identified the people you would like to have as mentors, it is time to do the approach. The approach I have seen work the best for me, and for the successful people I have come across in my podcast and throughout my life, is the "bring value" approach.

This is an approach in which you bring value to the table when you first approach your potential mentor with the intent of building a long-term, mutually beneficial relationship. You can bring value to them by offering something they need that you can offer. It might be offering to do some work for free, connecting them with someone they want to connect with, etc.

Don't make it formal and ask people if they want to become your mentor; that will only scare people away. Instead, offer to help them and ask them for the opportunity to learn from them. Be of service and be kind.

Start by asking them for coffee, as Alex suggests. Find out what is the best way to help them, offer your help, and ask them for advice on what you need help with. Put their advice in action and follow up with them, finding ways to build the relationship. Let the relationship grow organically. If you hit it off and both you and the mentor find value in the relationship, it will blossom.

Nowadays, you can also find virtual mentoring to complement your real life mentorship. You can find virtual from the best in the world and in any field by utilizing podcasts, books, You Tube videos, TED talks, seminars and conferences. There's no excuse to not get mentored as you can find it everywhere, with little effort, and at no cost to you.

I started the Logra Tu Dream podcast and I am writing this book to bring you virtual mentorship from successful Latinos and Latinas. I recognized that while I could find general business mentorship, I struggled to find it from the top Latinos and Latinas in this country.

But now you have access to mentorship from successful Latinos and Latinas, too, from Logra Tu Dream and from other emerging Latino podcasts and platforms.

So take action and get mentored. I can assure you it will bring tremendous value to your life and will help you as you pursue your quest to successfully live your dreams.

Join a Mastermind Group

"Dime con quien andas y te dire quien eres" (Tell me who you hang out with and I will tell you who you are)

-Old Mexican proverb

This is an old Mexican proverb which Nely Galan, Founder of the Adelante Movement, uses often to explain why you should always surround yourself with people who are better than you, because they will inspire you to improve yourself and be more like them. Instead of being jealous, you need to get inspired by people who are more successful than you. If you surround yourself with mediocrity, you will be mediocre. People tend to reflect and emulate the people they spend more time with, so aim high.

Mastermind groups are comprised of successful people who are committed to helping each other to achieve their dreams. Masterminds will inspire you, push you, and help you to get further faster. People who form and join mastermind groups are either successful people or people with a deep desire and commitment to become successful.

They have been an incredibly effective tool for top entrepreneurs. People like John Lee Dumas, Pat Flynn, Jaime Tardy and others credit masterminds as big contributors to their success.

Mastermind groups work because they bring together a group of highly-skilled and motivated people who work collectively to help you improve your skills and take your business and career to the next level. It is like being able to tap five minds instead of one when tackling problems or brainstorming new ideas. It also accelerates your learning, as you are exposed to a wealth of insights and experiences from many different walks of life.

A mastermind group will surround you with people who bring you new ideas, help you uncover new strategies for your business, help you get un-stuck, and who push you to be more and do more.

I joined the mastermind group "Fire Nation Elite" led by John Lee Dumas, one of the most successful business podcasters and online entrepreneurs out there. I joined when I decided to launch my podcast. I learned how to launch a successful podcast and was able to do so in just three months, in large part because of what I learned from almost 100 successful entrepreneurs and podcasters. I also built great relationships that continue to bring me value and opportunities.

This was a large mastermind group and it worked well because it was highly organized into smaller groups that would meet virtually every week to help members on a variety of different topics. Usually smaller masterminds work best; these can be groups of 5-7 people who connect once a week via Google hangouts or in person.

They have a structure that allows each person to get on the "hot seat" to discuss an important challenge they are facing, and the others chime in to offer advice and potential solutions.

For masterminds to work, all members must be committed to their own success and to the success of their mastermind colleagues. They must be willing to help and put in the time and effort it takes to become more successful, and commit to helping others do the same.

Sometimes it is hard to find likeminded people who are ahead of you in their lives, careers or business progression that you can mastermind with. This is why you need to join communities that can provide you with opportunities to meet these types of people.

There are a number of mastermind groups you can find out there, especially in the online entrepreneurial world, but I haven't come across one comprised of successful Latinos.

If you are looking to join a Latino mastermind group to take your life or career to the next level, let me know. I will be forming a network of motivated Latinos and Latinas like you who are looking for a community of likeminded people to propel their success.

All you need to do is sign up for our email list at www.logratudream.com/book and send me an email at: Arturo@logratudream.com, expressing interest in joining a mastermind.

Just put mastermind in the subject, tell me about yourself, what your dream is, and what you are looking to get out of and contribute to our mastermind group.

If there is enough interest, I will start the Logra Tu Dream mastermind group in which you can help each other out to improve your skills, knowledge and networks to create the life you want.

Just to say thanks for buying and reading my book, I would like to give you the Audiobook version 100% FREE! Go to: www.logratudream.com/freeaudiobook

Ask for help and get a Coach

"All of the wealthy people I have interviewed have a coach"

- Austin Netzley, Bestselling author of Make Money Live Wealthy and founder of Epic Launch

Wealthy and successful people understand the value of investing in themselves. This is why most of them have coaches they pay to help them improve their lives and their businesses. You would think that very successful people don't need much help and would be less likely to look for coaching versus less successful people. But the truth is actually the opposite; the most successful people are more successful precisely because they invest in themselves, and they keep investing throughout their lives.

Unsuccessful people are not successful because they don't invest in themselves. It is as simple as that. Sometimes they don't invest in themselves because they don't realize the importance of this, and because nobody has taught them to do so or showed them the benefits of self-investing.

It is very clear that the biggest asset we can use to reach our success and build wealth is our self. Also, it is very clear that investing in this asset to make it as effective as it can be will give you the best returns on your investment.

Coaching can reap huge dividends if you get the right coach. Having somebody who can help you achieve success and coach you so that you avoid big mistakes and maximize your potential can be life changing.

Go to your closest grocery store and ask the first three people you see if they would be willing to invest $500 a month in coaching that might change their lives, or if they would prefer to spend it on their dream car if they got a $500 per month raise tomorrow. I bet you at least two of them would choose the car. I have done this exercise myself and found that most prefer the car.

So why is it that most people would prefer the car, an asset that will quickly depreciate, instead of investing in coaching, which could give them the possibility to achieve their dreams?

This happens because of the perceived value most people assign to tangible things, which convey high social value like driving a great new car versus an intangible service that requires work to pay off. On one end, you drive off the lot with that dream car right away, getting immediate gratification.

On the other end, you know you will have to work very hard with a coach for a long period of time. You know your success will depend on whether you are able to act on what you learn, and that it will probably take time for you to see results from your hard work. You know that the pay off might be huge but in your mind it is uncertain and seems very far away.

So most people go for the sure thing that will bring them the short-term gratification but no long-term benefit instead of pursuing what seems a more uncertain long term huge pay off.

This is why very few people are very successful, because few people are willing to invest in themselves for the long term and have the willpower to forgo short-term rewards.

Action Items

- ✓ Understand the huge importance of getting mentored as it relates to achieving your dream
- ✓ Find mentors
- ✓ Get mentored
- ✓ Join a mastermind
- ✓ Get a coach

Chapter 11

BE A GIVER & SURROUND YOURSELF WITH PEOPLE THAT PULL YOU UP

"Give and you shall receive"

- Brendon Bruchard, best-selling author and leading entrepreneur

---

Nobody succeeds alone. Throughout my life and across my conversations with the more than 50 successful Latinos and Latinas I've interviewed, I have noticed that every one of them has surrounded themselves with the right people.

By "right people" I mean a supportive network of other positive, successful people who are working hard to accomplish their own dreams. These types of people are also givers.

In life there are matchers, givers and takers. Matchers will go tit for tat, helping you if you help them. Givers will help you without expecting anything in return, and takers will only take without giving back.

You need to surround yourself with givers who are positive, successful people with an abundance mindset, and who are kind and understand that we only succeed if we help each other. These people will help you on your journey to success.

You must also avoid takers as soon as you identify them. Takers will ask for your help but will not reciprocate. They will try to tear you down many times and leave you with a bad taste in your mouth. Once you identify a taker, run as fast as you can. You will not be able to change a taker into a giver. Takers will just suck the life out of you and leave you disappointed.

So it is best to literally take the takers out of your life.

Givers will help you get what you want. BUT to be able to attract givers to your life who support you in your journey, you must be a giver too.

Start by helping these givers out however you are able to. It can be as simple as sharing their social media posts, connecting them with other people, giving them advice, etc.

Give in a way that is fulfilling to you so that you don't burn out. This means giving within your means in terms of available time and resources, and to people and causes that inspire you and you feel deserve your help. If you give too much and sacrifice yourself and your family in the process, you will resent the giving and it will burn you out.

"If we don't start helping each other out, nobody else is gonna do it"

- Tayde Aburto, Founder Hispanic Chamber of e-commerce

Tayde Aburto is the founder of the Hispanic Chamber of e-commerce, a social enterprise using the power of business to get Hispanic-owned businesses online and to help them to become more competitive by using the Internet as a business tool. Through hard work, he has built a successful organization that helps Latino family businesses succeed.

When I interviewed him on the Logra Tu Dream podcast, we talked about the biggest challenge that Latino business owners face. He was very clear: it is their own mindset.

Tayde talked about how many times he has experienced Latino business owners seeing other Latino business owners as their biggest competition when in fact they could be their biggest source of support.

"We need to help each other to create businesses in this great nation that is the US"

- Mauricio Simbeck, CEO Milagros de México

Many Latino business owners don't understand that if they help each other, they make the pie larger for everybody involved and they all win.

As a consequence, many don't collaborate with each other. In fact, many times they try to tear each other down. Because of this, many Latino and Latina business owners don't succeed like they should because they don't build the support network that is essential to success.

"I hope that successful Hispanic entrepreneurs contribute back to the community. It is not just about building wealth; there has to be a purpose."

- Fidel Vargas CEO of Hispanic Scholarship Fund

We need to shift our mindset to one of giving and collaboration and understand that if we focus on helping each other instead of tearing each other down, we will thrive.

Tayde is on a mission to help Latino small business owners understand how they can all get new business if they cross-promote each other. There are 3.2 million Latino-owned businesses in the US, 75 percent of which are small family businesses.

Tayde saw that there weren't other Latino organizations helping these types of businesses and he put it on himself and his organization to fill this gap.

"The only way we can accomplish something greater in the family business sector is by helping each other out. The more you help, the more that you give back, [and] the easier it is gonna be for you to accomplish your goals," says Tayde.

In a previous chapter, I talked about how the Indian and Jewish communities collaborate very well, helping those who need help, and they have become incredibly successful by doing so. I see a future where we spark a movement in which many entrepreneurs in our Latino community are inspired to help each other succeed.

Building a Strong Network

Mahrinah Von Schlegel understands well the importance of strong and broad networks in entrepreneurial success. She is a very successful entrepreneur, anthropologist, and ecosystem builder who has founded various entrepreneurial ecosystems by building a strong and very large support network by giving. She is a super connector, and believes that the key to success is to approach other people who can help you by helping them yourself:

"Build a very strong network, reach out to everyone yourself, follow up and connect. Meet them in person; be very strategic about how to grow your network based on where you don't have a lot of reach. Say yes when people ask for help and try to be as authentic and helpful as possible. A lot of people want to build a network but don't want to give back and this is not how this works."

Once you connect with new people, you need to build strong relationships. To build strong relationships, you need to socialize with people you work with so that people know that you can be trusted and so that you know whom you can trust.

People will not just measure the quality of your work but, more importantly, they will measure your quality as a person. So you need to spend time getting to know the people you work with socially to build the relationships that will allow you to become successful in your career, whether you have a job or whether you are an entrepreneur.

Successful Business Networking

Luis O. de La Hoz is the Senior Vice President of the Lending Team at the Intersect Fund, a non-profit, micro-lender and certified CDFI based in New Brunswick. He is the chair of the Central New Jersey Small Business Council of the Middlesex County Regional Chamber of Commerce.

De la Hoz is also a member of BNI International Hawks Chapter, a group of professionals working together to build business and referrals, where he won the Notable Networker Award in 2010, 2011 and 2012 in recognition of outstanding team performance, referrals, visitors and closed business.

Luis is a master business networker and has identified the three stages of successful business networking:

1. **Visibility:** Become visible so you attract more people to your sphere.
2. **Credibility:** Once you are visible then you can build your credibility, and if your credibility is good enough, people will start recommending you based on it.
3. **Harvesting:** Over time, if you build relationships with your business network and bring value to them, your efforts will yield you increasingly more business.

Luis has taken this approach to the next level. He has built his personal board of advisors comprised of the right people who can help him become more successful. He meets with his personal board of advisors every week for two hours. This group has become an invaluable source of advice and provides connections that have helped him thrive.

Grow your influence on social media

Latinos and Latinas are avid social media consumers but most do not use it to build their businesses. Social media can bring you visibility with the people you want to establish credibility with. So it is very important to learn how to use social media to build your business.

Make sure your social media profiles are customer friendly. Present yourself and your business in a professional manner, avoiding any content that might scare away customers.

Make sure you connect with your network with social media, and make a point of helping them out as much as you can by sharing their posts and by offering encouragement, information and advice.

I find that Twitter works great for me; I have built relationships with a number of very prominent influencers in the Latino community as well as in the online entrepreneur and podcasting community. The more I help people, the more I get back, and the more I engage with great people on social media, the more I grow my circle of influence.

Build your Tribe

Seth Godin, who in my opinion is one of the most brilliant marketing minds of our time, introduced the concept of building your tribe in one of his best-selling books *Tribes*.

A tribe is a community of people united by common aspirations, values and purpose. Tribes follow a leader and band together to help each other accomplish their missions. Tribes are engaged communities of people with similar needs and problems. Tribe members join tribes to look for help in a number of different arenas: entrepreneurial businesses, arts, sports, etc.

Anyone building any type of business or platform that serves people who identify with groups will benefit from building a tribe. In other words, everybody can benefit from building a tribe.

Build an email list of your tribe

"Offer people what they want, not what you think they need"

- Maritza Parra, Entrepreneur, Speaker and Podcaster extraordinaire

As you build your network and attract people to your business, you must build an email list so that you can strengthen your relationship with them by adding value to their lives. To set up an email list, you'll need a Mail Chimp account and you'll want to connect it to the App Sumo plug-in on your website.

To get people to sign up to your list, you will need to offer them a free gift that provides them relevant value to their lives. Many call this gift the lead magnet. Let's say you are an online entrepreneur in the health and wellness arena. In this case, your lead magnet might be a one-page pdf with the top 10 habits of healthy people; it might be a video series or even a book.

In the last few years, an industry has literally come out of the woodwork to teach people how to build email lists that you can leverage to grow profitable businesses online. A simple search will reveal an endless list of online marketing experts in this field. You can quickly be overwhelmed and flooded with information.

But like with anything in life, there are always some people who rise to the top of their fields. If you want to learn how to build your email list, I highly recommend you check out Jeff Walker's book, *Launch*, and Lewis Howes' webinar course.

Jeff will teach you how to use the sideways sales letter to build a successful business around your email list. The sideways sales letter is a three-part video series that teaches people about a specific topic leading them to a paid course,

122

product or subscription service. Jeff has helped countless entrepreneurs make literally hundreds of millions of dollars using this proven method.

Lewis Howes' webinar course uses the webinar method to do the same. His webinar teaches people about a certain topic, leading them to buy a paid course, subscription service or product. The webinar has proven to be an incredibly powerful method to building your email list and getting your tribe to buy what they want from you.

John Lee Dumas has built a $3 million per year business in large part due to his effective use of webinars to sell subscriptions to Podcasters Paradise, the #1 podcasting community online that teaches people how to create, grow, and monetize their podcast.

Maritza Parra teaches people to grow their email list so that they can get more clients, help more people, and make more money. Maritza is the best in her field and I highly recommend you check her out if you want to learn how to build your email list/tribe.

As you build your list, you can reach out to your subscribers and share content that is helpful and builds trust with them. Once they know, like, and trust you, they will be ready to buy from you. Remember, people buy from other people who they know, like and trust.

Always ask your tribe what they want from you and make it easy for them to buy. Make offers and learn what they want by asking. Once you know what your community wants and have a relationship with them, develop a product or service around what they want and offer it to them.

Chances are pretty good that people who know, like, and trust you will buy what they have told you they want. Make sure you deliver exceptional value to your community in anything you sell to them or give them for free.

By continuously giving value to your tribe, they will feel very grateful to you and continue to follow you and buy from you. On the other hand, if you don't provide enough value to your tribe, they will stop following you and you will not be very successful building a business around your tribe.

Action Steps

- ✓ Be a Giver.
- ✓ Surround yourself with people more successful than you, who can help you get what you want, and who are also givers.
- ✓ Take Takers out of your life.
- ✓ Build your network by helping others, by being authentic and by proactively connecting with key people in your field.
- ✓ Build meaningful relationships with your network based on trust, respect and reciprocity.
- ✓ Expand your circle of influence through social media.
- ✓ Build your tribe by giving them value and keep in touch with them by building your email list.

Chapter 12

BRING YOUR UNIQUE VALUE TO THE MARKETPLACE

"You got to start thinking for yourself. We are all beautifully individual; there is so much that makes us uniquely our own. But we don't do a good job exploring the full extent of that potential; we become complacent, fitting in what everything is supposed to be. We are just absorbing the opinion of others through osmosis and ignorance is spreading through us like a really bad virus."

— Raymmar Tirado, artist, digital strategist, creative explorer of ideas and founder of Raymmar.com

125

Find your uniqueness and mission

We all have a gift inside of us and our responsibility is to share it with the world. When we are able to unearth our gift and share, we reach the maximum expression of ourselves. When we don't, the fire inside us is extinguished.

There is nobody on earth like you: you are a unique being with something wonderful to offer the world. You have experience, personality, beliefs, skills and spirit that nobody else has.

You also have a mission, whether you have identified it or not. You have a purpose that your soul wants to fulfill in this life. The mission is what tugs at your heart and makes its presence felt in your gut. It's like a hidden force trying to guide you to what will make you truly happy and fulfilled.

Sometimes we recognize our mission and embrace it, and sometimes we don't. If you do as all the Latinos and Latinas I have interviewed, you will find your success. If you don't find it or if you bury it, it will extinguish the fire you have inside you, leaving a deep hole in your soul. It will haunt you throughout your life, because when you feel its call and ignore it, this will create sadness, anger and regret.

"Sometimes what you think is your biggest weakness is your biggest strength"

- Deldelp Medina, CEO Avion Ventures and Co-Founder Latino Startup Alliance

It is hard to find and embrace our own uniqueness. It is hard because society trains us to conform, to be and think like everybody else. Since childhood, we learned that if we stand out, we'll get picked on at school. As we grew up, we learned that if we are to succeed, we need to conform to the norms of society.

We learned that we needed to go to college and get a good job. Once in the workforce, we learned the rules we needed to follow to "get ahead." We were evaluated in large measure based on how we followed these rules:

Don't be yourself and communicate what you really feel because you'll get in trouble. Don't think differently and challenge the status quo. Don't be too original because you will not fit in, etc...

What this indoctrination creates is group think, in which people conform to the norm because of the fear that if they are different they will get punished and not get ahead. We get home from work and turn on the TV, where we are bombarded by negativity, irrelevant gossip and TV ads for products that most of the time will not make us healthy or wealthy (soda, junk food, cars, etc.).

The old media wants us to watch more TV so they can sell more ads to advertisers so we can consume more of what they are selling to us. They focus on negative news stories because we are wired psychologically to pay more attention when we feel fear and anxiety. They focus on selling you the idea that in order to be successful you need to buy more stuff, look like the celebrity images you see, etc.

They are selling you the idea that to be successful you need to be like everybody else, which could not be further from reality.

With all these negative influences and the indoctrination to conform, to be scared, and to follow, it is tough to find your uniqueness and even tougher to embrace it. This is why, in order to find your uniqueness, you need to turn off the TV and learn to recognize when they are trying to sell you or indoctrinate you.

Think independently because if you don't you will be living somebody else's life. If you live somebody else's life, you will not find yourself and unearth your gift. Resist the temptation to conform, as conforming leads to mediocrity.

People who conform don't come up with original ideas; they don't take risks, and they haven't summoned the courage to pursue their calling. They are not willing to make the hard choices, put in the work, and endure the pain that comes with pushing through the difficult barriers that hold them back.

The market has one rule: it rewards value.

The highest value you can create in this world is to express your uniqueness in pursuit of your mission. Your uniqueness is comprised of your skills, life experience, passion, ideas and personality.

It combines passion and contribution.

"We were not intended to hate our jobs; you gotta free yourself."

— Raymmar Tirado, artist, digital strategist, creative explorer of ideas and founder of Raymmar.com

It is important to find your uniqueness because it will lead you to your mission, and by fulfilling your mission, you will become the highest expression of yourself.

To find your uniqueness, you must find your strengths. To do this, you need to first listen more to your gut and capture

128

what you are learning about yourself. Make a running list with two columns of the following. Fill the left column with the answers aligned with your mission and the right column with the answers that are not aligned with your mission. This will be your "uniqueness balance sheet":

Aligned	Not Aligned
If money were no object, what would you do?	Conversely, what would you never do, even if you were offered all the money in the world?
Which problems are you deeply passionate about solving?	Which problems do you want to avoid because you know you will be miserable if you try to solve them?
What makes you happy?	What makes you unhappy?
What fills you with energy?	What drains you?
What drives you to work incessantly?	What makes you procrastinate incessantly?
What can you do well and effortlessly, that brings value to others?	What do you struggle with and is drudgery to you?
Ask friends, family and work colleagues you trust about what they see as your biggest strengths?	What do they see as your biggest weaknesses?
What visions of yourself bring you immense happiness and fulfillment?	Which visions of yourself bring you fear anxiety and sadness?

✓ Take the Strengths Finder 2.0 test that you will find in the hard copy of the *Strengths Finder 2.0* book and learn what your biggest strengths are.

These are the clues your soul is giving you about what your uniqueness and your mission are. Do this over a consistent period of time, adding to the list as you identify these answers until your strengths and your mission become clear to you.

Build on your strengths

"Hone that edge, just wax on wax off. You have to become that expert, 10,000 hours baby! People want to be good but so many people don't want to put in the work to be good."

- Raymmar Tirado

First, build on your strengths. You can't be the best at something that doesn't leverage your biggest strengths. You will tend to like what you are good at, and be motivated to work hard to master the craft. On the other hand, you will not like what you are not good at.

Raymmar Tirado is a creative and controversial thinker who believes that thinking for yourself is the key to finding your uniqueness. By doing an inner exploration and setting out on a quest to learn more, letting go of preconceived notions, he has found his calling and his success.

Raymmar was a college dropout who could not find real work. He was an insurance salesman when the economy went south and things fell apart for him. His life was falling apart; he went through the pain of divorce and financial troubles. The combination of all this led to a breaking point.

He ended up moving back to live in his mother's basement for a couple of years, working what he calls "sweat shop sales" jobs to climb out of the deep hole he was in. He found himself working very hard for other people and he kept asking himself, "Where is the pay off? What am I building for myself?"

He realized that if he was going to work that hard selling door-to-door to dozens of places a day; he might as well work that hard for himself.

He discovered that people kept buying because they liked and trusted him, and they realized his good intentions to help them. He found that he was a terrific salesman, with a unique and superior approach. He also realized that he was an independent thinker who could add significant value to the world by sharing these thoughts. He had found his strengths.

He realized that if he just came up with a product that was him, and develop a system around the way he was successfully selling, he could replicate the process at scale and fundamentally shift the world of sales. Raymmar had found his mission and he pursued this business idea, starting his own online platform, raymmar.com.

He is building a system that creates value for his clients' consumers which in turn rewards their clients with their business. He pushes his clients to tell stories that capture their consumers emotionally, stories of the people who work with them, like the one of the single mother working two jobs to provide for her kids. Stories like this one engage consumers emotionally.

Raymmar leads his clients to create a community of these engaged users and then tap into their influence to build the business. This he calls the "currency of influence," which has proven to be very successful.

His system helps many companies grow their business, saving them marketing costs that they are then able to invest back in product development and employee benefits. Raymmar's platform had over 3.5 million page views in the last year, attracting over 11K email subscribers and top clients like Keller Williams Realty and iCompass, among many others.

The way to increase your influence today is by building your own platform. Your platform is a representation of the unique value that only you can offer the world. Your platform takes your mission to the next level.

Raymmar's provocative platform is composed of:

- Mission: Revolutionize the world of sales and shed light on what he sees as the truth in business, life, love and liberty.
- Content that creates value in people's lives: blog, podcast, videos and articles on his website and other platforms (Huffington Post, Medium, You Tube, etc.) focused on shedding the truth about controversial topics.
- Business that solves a problem: his sales and content marketing system/business with which he serves clients by helping them sell more and save money.
- An engaged community that wields the currency of influence.

His online platform is not just about his business; he also shares his unique perspectives on business, life, love and liberty. Raymmar has built a business and a platform crafted around his uniqueness. The uniqueness of the system he came up with is based on his own experience and skills, as well as the uniqueness of his thoughts on life, love and liberty.

It is a platform that represents the highest expression of who Raymmar really is. It creates significant value to the world in a way that no one can, except Raymmar. No one can replicate Raymmar's platform because there is only one

Raymmar Tirado in this world, so in this regard he has no competition. Raymmar has created his own monopoly. Will you create yours?

Action Steps

✓ Think for yourself and see reality for what it really is.
✓ Avoid media manipulation.
✓ Do your uniqueness balance sheet to find your uniqueness and identify your strengths.
✓ Build on your strengths, honing that edge, "wax on-wax off."
✓ Create your own monopoly.

Chapter 13

MASTER THE ONE THREAD YOU CAN DO BETTER THAN ANYBODY ELSE

"Do what you can and can the rest"

- David Gomez, President & CEO of David Gomez and Associates

Weave and Then Master Your ONE Thread

According to James Altucher, the author of *Choose Yourself*, the average person has 14 different careers in their lives, and the average multi-millionaire has seven different sources of income. James argues that teaching kids to focus on the one job they want to have when they grow up will create a generation of kids who will learn the hard way that life doesn't work like that.

James is right. In today's world and in the future, it will not be about mastering ONE job or skill. It will be about mastering ONE "thread" that connects and combines your mission, your unique set of skills, talents, experiences, and your work.

This ONE thread is the unique combination of these factors that will help differentiate you from others, and what you will need to become a master at.

For me, this ONE thread is being a brand builder, a community leader and a creator in the Latino world. My mission to help others achieve their dreams, my brand building skills and experience, my deep knowledge of the Latino community, my Logra Tu Dream podcast, my book, and my speaking all combine and connect to form this thread.

All these components build on each other. The more I grow my brand building skills, the stronger my Logra Tu Dream platform becomes, the better leader I become, and the stronger the ONE thread becomes.

To find and weave your ONE thread, you need to follow your mission, NOT your passion. Your mission is about what you can contribute to the world. Your passion is what you are excited about right now.

Fernanda Chacon's mission is to create a consciousness around how nutrition and exercise impacts people in a positive or negative way; not only in their weight, but also in their attitude, growth, health, and lifestyle.

To pursue her mission, she started her *Cook and Move* blog and video platform, and authored *Heavenly Skinny Kitchen*, becoming an award-winning nutritionist, health coach, blogger & TV co-host. She has been featured on Univision, Mundo Fox, and TeleChicago.

She has dedicated herself to creating and revamping recipes for new, healthy and balanced dishes without restricting food groups, but instead focusing on better options without processed foods.

Through her *Cook and Move* platform and her "Cooking and Moving for Success" campaign. She trains and educates others in how to lead a more pleasant, healthy lifestyle with good nutrition and proper movement.

Fernanda has woven and is mastering her ONE thread as an authority in healthy eating and living in the Latino community by pursuing her mission of creating a consciousness around how nutrition and exercise impacts people. Her ONE thread connects and combines her blog, her You Tube video channel, her coaching, her work as a nutritionist, and her TV co-hosting.

Your mission is enduring because it is why you are here in this world, and because it comes from your soul. Your passion is ephemeral because it comes from a more superficial place: what you like today will not be the same as what you like in 20 years.

To weave and master your ONE thread, focus on what you do well and apply it towards your journey in fulfilling your mission. As you progress, focus on mastery through continuous and relentless practice. As Arnold Schwarzenegger says, you need to put in the reps.

You will help many people and you will be incredibly fulfilled during the process.

It is very important that you weave and then master your ONE thread throughout your career and your life, with intent so that you are bringing your unique value to the world. Don't drift because drifting does not lead to mastery; it doesn't lead anywhere.

Mastering your ONE thread will bring you your maximum expression of success because it is based on creating value with what you can uniquely offer the world. And this is something you can do better than anyone else...

Find a problem that you deeply desire to solve and fill the gap

"Find a need and fill the gap"
                    - Manny Ruiz, Founder Hispanicize

Manny Ruiz's American Dream was to build something successful that would provide for his family, but he didn't know what it would be.

He learned early on that a key trait that many successful people shared was that they found a need and filled the gap. So he always tried to be unique and different in his quest to find his own niche. He didn't have the idea of becoming an entrepreneur when he started his journey. He wanted to be an NFL football player but that didn't pan out. He has always loved film, and even though this is something he has not yet pursued, his dream is much alive.

He backed into becoming an entrepreneur. He started his journey with a business failure in which he learned three valuable lessons that have enabled him to be successful: be focused, have a marketing plan, and know what you are doing.

In the late 90's in the midst of the dotcom boom, he was the leader of a PR agency's Hispanic practice. He worked with many young people who had startups; many with bad ideas but they were being funded by investors. He realized that he could do something like that and start his own company.

He saw that it was very difficult for professionals, marketing agencies and major brands to reach the Hispanic media. He found a need and decided to fill the gap with a company that would provide Hispanic press release wire services.

Experiment Your Way to Your Success

He continued to apply the "find the need and fill the gap" principle with his business, launching various services. In 2003, he launched the first network of Hispanic newspapers online, *Hispanic Digital Network*. He built alliances with Hispanic newspapers across the US and gave them a free digital publishing platform. This was a huge advantage in 2003, back before the Word Press era.

They hosted the newspaper websites and allowed them to advertise in them. They had exclusive agreements with Hispanic publishers so when they distributed the press release, they would also put the press releases with photos and even videos on the Hispanic Digital Network. The newspapers had to have exclusive rights with Manny's network to do their newsfeeds so they ended up becoming the first true online Hispanic media network.

In 2007 he sold Hispanic Digital Network, Hispanic PR wire, and Latin Clips, his three core businesses, to the parent company of PR News Wire for $5.5 million. Manny has always had a blue-collar mindset and has been underestimated many times, so this was a very special accomplishment for himself and his family.

He went to work for the company that acquired his companies but only a year later he was bored out of his mind and decided to moonlight to figure out what he wanted to do next. During the day, he went to work and at night he worked for a year on a project to build a movie theater with film, fun and food, spending $90K of his own money.

The project did not come to fruition, as investors were staying away from commercial real estate in 2009 and he could not land the funding he needed to make it a reality. So he continued to experiment and in 2009 he launched the Hispanic PR blog, writing about Hispanic PR and social media. But he realized he would not make any money with the blog.

At the end of 2009, he continued his experiments, coming up with the idea of launching the first ever national event for the Hispanic PR industry. The conference was called the Hispanic PR and Social Media Conference. He partnered with the Hispanic Public Relations Association, who had no national footprint.

His first event had over 200 attendees, but the experience sucked the blood out of him and he found that a PR-only conference didn't make any money.

But soon he got exposed to the SXSW conference in Austin. At that moment, he got the idea of changing the name of the conference to Hispanicize. He also realized that if he broadened the conference from PR to bloggers, it would be a

140

huge success, because he knew the blogosphere was about to explode.

He faced significant resistance to these changes but he pushed through the skepticism, following his gut. The first conference in 2010 was a big success. In 2011 he brought in filmmakers, and in 2013 he included the music industry and journalists. By 2014, Hispanicize established itself as the top Hispanic event for bloggers, journalist and marketers.

I was fortunate enough to be at Hispanicize 2015, where it cemented its place as a world-class event, transcending the boundaries of the Latino world.

Today Hispanicize is the biggest Hispanic marketing and blogging event, and the second biggest Hispanic journalist event in the nation. It has become a full-scale, multi-industry event in which trendsetters from these industries in the Hispanic world converge. People keep coming back to Hispanicize because they know that if they don't they will miss something huge.

Manny feels that he needs to earn people's respect every day to continue to be successful. Hispanicize is the product of building success on top of a previous success, of leveraging previous wins to build the next thing. People believe Manny when he tells them that the next Hispanicize will be bigger than the previous year. They believe him because he has over-delivered every single year.

Manny has experimented his way toward finding the ONE thread that he does better than anybody else: becoming one of the top Latino entrepreneurs and influencers in the US.

He started out not knowing where his path would lead. But by following his gut, and finding the gaps to problems he deeply cared about and filling them, he has found and mastered his domain.

In the process, he has built Hispanicize, which has blossomed not only into the top event in the Latino world but also into the largest privately-owned social media community in the nation. Hispanicize owns Dime Media, one of the biggest Latina bloggers networks, and Hispanic PR wire, an innovative PR wire service which combines social media with PR at a lower cost. Hispanicize also has a stake in Being Latino, the biggest Latino Facebook community with 4.4 million fans.

He accomplished his success by outworking everybody, and he attributes his success to his faith in God. His faith has given him the inspiration to dream big and believe in miracles. When people told him his ideas were crazy, he knew he was on to something and pressed on to make what seemed impossible a reality.

To experiment potential career directions that you think you might like, reach out to people thriving in those careers. Get a good sense of what they do and what drives their success. If possible, shadow them to experience first-hand what it is like to be in their shoes.

As you learn what your strengths are and what potential directions might be a good fit for you, narrow it down, take action, and choose a path. Choose the right industry for you, find the need and fill the gap, building your niche in the process like Manny did.

The Path to Mastery: Practice and Perseverance

"Be very persistent and understand that rejection is part of the process and of your development. There is no substitute

for ganas (wanting it), energy, enthusiasm and effort. It doesn't exist."
- Gaby Natale, President Super Latina TV

To become a master in any craft, you need to put in the reps over many years of hard work. Malcolm Gladwell in his book *Outlier* talks about the 10K hour rule. He has found through his research that you can reach the top 5% of any profession if you devote 10K hours to practicing the craft with intention.

Gaby Natale went from being unemployed in Argentina to the president of her own media company and studio: Super Latina TV. She achieved this through persistence and putting in the reps over more than a decade.

She started her journey by finding a job as a translator and an assistant at a conference in Mexico. The same people who had invited her to the conference in Mexico reached out to her with a job opportunity in the US in the PR industry.

Despite experiencing abuse in the workplace, she decided not to do anything about it. She didn't want to lose her job, and she wanted to preserve her dream of owning her own media company someday. She continued to build experience, finding a job as a TV news anchor at a television station in Texas. She came up with the idea of a TV program that would feature inspirational stories targeted at Latinas and she quit her job to pursue it.

With only a PowerPoint presentation, she convinced a TV channel owner in Midland-Odessa, Texas to give her a chance to air her show on his channel. She didn't have a TV program yet but through hustle and with the help of the Small Business Administration, she managed to get a loan from a credit union, despite having no credit history, which allowed her to start Super Latina TV.

They started to create the TV show in a rug storage facility. To make her dream a reality, she invested in learning her craft, which involved not only production, but sales and marketing, too. She first started with minimal equipment and resources but she perfected her craft, always finding ways to improve the quality of her program through practice.

She focused on her core capabilities and delegated the rest. Soon her clients were calling, asking her to develop TV ads, activations, and videos to market their brands.

She was nominated six times to the Emmy awards; she expanded to include the Gaby Natale and Super Latina TV You Tube channels, which have 30 million total views and is growing at the rate of 1 million views per month. The incredible success of her YouTube channel helped convince VME to distribute her TV program nationally in 43 markets in the US, Puerto Rico and now in Canada.

Gaby proves that you don't need to come from money or start with knowing everything to be successful. Her keys to success are to be persistent, to never give up, and to understand that failure and rejection is part of the process. She used rejection as a way to learn what she needed to improve at her craft, and failure became her best teacher, helping her achieve an incredible level of success. Gaby has learned that there is no substitute to effort (ganas), and enthusiasm.

Gaby has become a master of her craft; she is a master TV presenter, a top Latina influencer, and a super successful media entrepreneur. She has risen to the top of her profession, attracting top celebrities like Deepak Chopra, Carlos Santana, Thalia, Cristina Saralegui, and William Levy, among many others to her show.

When she first started her path, she had no experience in what it took to build a successful media company or how to be a master presenter and top influencer. Gaby mastered these crafts in the twelve years since she arrived in the US. With her boundless enthusiasm, she took action, learning from failure and always finding ways to improve.

She is an inspiration and an example of how to become the master of your domain through hustle, practice, and hard work. If you have the pleasure of meeting Gaby, you will see how she brings to life that inspirational Mexican phrase "Si se puede."

Master your Niche

"There is a great satisfaction in trying and creating: If you are not successful at the first or second try, you will be successful at the third or fourth try. If you continue trying, you will eventually achieve it; you just have to have a lot of perseverance."
- Mauricio Simbeck, CEO Milagros de Mexico

Mauricio Simbeck is the co-founder and CEO of Milagros de Mexico, a retail chain that sells health and wellness products to the Latino Community, with five stores located in established Hispanic neighborhoods in San Francisco, San Jose, Oakland and Redwood City. Milagros de Mexico was one of 12 recipients of the prestigious Chase Mission Main St grant awarded to outstanding small business nationwide.

Mauricio has become a master of the Hispanic retail business. He started as a small business owner in Mexico, and then came to Harvard Business School to study his MBA. After his MBA he worked for HEB, a top retail chain with more than 300 stores, many of them serving Hispanic consumers. He worked for HEB for six years where he learned the retail craft. From the importance of planning and

145

analyzing the business, to leading and motivating people, he learned how the retail business worked at HEB.

Then he started his first entrepreneurial venture, a membership club targeted to the Hispanic community. The business didn't work out but it cemented his passion for helping the Hispanic community. He realized the huge need for educating Latinos about how to lead healthier lives. After this experience, he joined the Farmacias Remedios executive team, a Hispanic retail drugstore, where he continued learning the Hispanic retail business. The 2008 crisis hit Farmacias Remedios hard but they were able to sell the company.

After Farmacias Remedios, he started Milagros de Mexico, another retail company focused on helping the Hispanic community to lead healthier lives through health products and education. Mauricio is passionate about helping bring health to the Latino community and has continued to perfect his craft throughout his career.

He started the Milagros de Mexico health products brand to offer natural products to help Hispanics manage diseases like diabetes and to lose weight. He also offers natural beauty products.

He has built mastery in managing a retail business that serves the Hispanic market and in the sales and marketing of health products and education. He has done so by learning as an employee of a large company, an executive of a small company and as an entrepreneur.

Mauricio has learned that the keys to success in his business are to treat his employees well so that they treat consumers well, and to relentlessly focus on what his consumers want.

He has continued to focus on his niche to become the best in his field. If you look up the top retail executives in the Hispanic health products business in the US, Mauricio's name will surely come up.

Action Steps

- ✓ Weave and master the ONE thread that connects and combines your mission, your unique set of skills, your talents, your experiences and your work.
- ✓ Find a problem you deeply desire to solve and fill the gap.
- ✓ Experiment your way to your success.
- ✓ Practice, practice, practice.
- ✓ Be persistent.
- ✓ Master your niche.

Chapter 14

BECOME A CREATOR, NOT A CONSUMER

"We have to change the idea of being only passive consumers to becoming creators. We buy more mobile phones, we spend more time online and on social media, but we are not creators at the level we can be."

-Deldelp Medina, CEO of Avion Ventures and Co-Founder Latino Startup Alliance

Being a consumer doesn't maximize our potential; it drains our resources to make others wealthy. Many times we buy things we don't need to impress people we don't like with money we don't have.

Consumers spend their money chasing the mirage that marketers paint for them. This is the kind of mirage that tells the middle-aged guy that if he buys that new sports car, he will transform himself into a cool guy who is sought after by beautiful women.

It uses our hard-earned money to build someone else's dream, not yours. It keeps us stuck because we are not creating the value we are capable of. Instead, it drains our limited resources so we don't progress. We might feel great with that new car for the first few months after we buy, it but it doesn't transform us into the person we wanted to become when we purchased it.

We knew it was a mirage but we bought it, anyway because we wanted to escape and dream for a little bit. Instead, we need to be willing to put in the hard work and the pain it takes to achieve our deep aspirations. The path to achieving your dreams will inevitably transform you into a creator.

Because the market has one simple rule: It rewards the creators of value.

Our community comprises a huge market coveted by the biggest companies in the world. They spend billions trying to get us to buy the products and services they sell.

We are seen as consumers who are to be targeted so they can win a share of our wallets. But if we are to reach our potential we need to become creators: creators of solutions, new businesses, art, new products and services that serve others.

Creating is leaving your mark on the world; it is letting your gift out. It is being fulfilled.

What the world wants is YOU

Becoming a creator gives us the opportunity to control our own destiny. To start that business we have been thinking about. To start that blog or that podcast, to write that book we have inside us. It means shaping our environment, our culture; it means not accepting what they push on us.

Seize The Latino Market Opportunity

"The Latino market is not an incremental opportunity that clients can think about for their business; it is absolutely a business imperative. If you are a marketer today in California and you are not marketing to US Hispanics, then you are not marketing to California."
- Sandra Alfaro, Managing Partner Wing Agency

Sandra Alfaro is the managing partner for the Wing agency, one of the top multicultural agencies in the country. She started her career in the Latino market 20 years ago. Sandra thought it was a great time to be in the Latino market 20 years ago and she still thinks the same way today.

She has worked with some of the biggest brands in the country: Wal-Mart, Heineken USA, McDonald's, Sprint, The Home Depot, JCPenney's, Kraft Foods, Nissan, Wendy's, P&G, just to name a few. She has seen how her clients, who are some of the biggest companies in the country, are realizing that most if not all of their US growth is going to come from the multicultural Latino consumer.

The Latino market is incredibly attractive for companies across the economy. It is very attractive because we are 54

151

million strong, representing $1.5 trillion in spending power and 60% of US population growth5. Contrary to what many believe, the Latino market is not a marginal, low-income market.

In fact, affluent Hispanics who are young, urban and connected are on the rise. There are about 15 million affluent Latinos in the US; they represent 27% of the Latino population and about 37% of the Latino spending power6.

They are working hard to realize their American Dream. They are in white-collar jobs, have a robust entrepreneurial spirit, and are avid consumers of technology, upscale products, health foods, travel and more.

There has been explosive growth in emerging Hispanic markets driven by domestic migration of Hispanics. This migration will result in a greater increase in Latin influence and greater diversity in these markets.

The Mainstream is Under the Latin Influence

Not only is the Latino market very attractive for businesses, but we are also changing the fabric of America. We are changing politics, food, fashion, business, and art.

Latino culture is having a tremendous influence on mainstream America. This influence is reflected in mainstream consumers who are adopting Latino purchasing habits, beliefs and attitudes. Popular culture, politics, food, fashion, art, marketing, brands and products are being infused with and inspired by Latino culture.

This culture is very influential because the Latin world offers some of the most fascinating, beautiful and flavorful inspiration in the world, and because it is being spread via social media. Latinos love it and most Americans that have experienced it love it, too.

According to the "Latino Influence Project" study done by Experian Simmons and Wing in 2012, Latinos are influencing non-Latinos living around them, not only on the above aspects but also on things like perception of success, technology, attitudes towards family, and religion.

Retro-Acculturation

Retro-acculturation is the process by which Latinos, after going through acculturation, revert to their original culture as they yearn to connect with their Latino roots.

This is a fairly new phenomenon among young Hispanic adults. In fact, this is even seen among third- and fourth-generation Hispanics, where they are seeking an emotional connection that combines both U.S. culture and their family's original culture. They retro-acculturate by embracing Latino values at a deeper level than before.

They become interested in various types of Latin foods and dishes from their childhood, or they seek to establish a previously non-existing connection to their heritage.

This re-awakening of their culture is driving Latinos to look for and engage in authentic Latino experiences that will bring a sense of connection to their traditions. There is a tremendous opportunity for culturally authentic brand and product experiences.

Latina Moms

Latina moms are the primary shoppers in their household, controlling the bulk of the family spending.

Most of them happen to be Millennials who bring with them their cultural tastes, experiences and expectations, which are at times different from their older Latina moms and non-Latina peers.

Eighty-seven percent of them see themselves as both Latinas and American; they are embracing the two worlds they live in. Her family is everything and she cares deeply about her community and her culture. She is a big believer in education and is committed to trying to provide the best education for her children.

This unique cultural background and series of "firsts" in terms of education, income and confidence provides marketers with tremendous business opportunities.

The brands that conquer the heart of Latina moms will be incredibly successful.

The Future Opportunities in the Latino Market

We are integrated into the fabric of America. This is why companies are now devising new approaches to go after this new integrated market. They call it the "Total Market Approach" but what is clear is that if they don't succeed with Latinos, they don't succeed, period.

Sandra sees a future in which the minority groups will become the majority and in which mainstream marketing will become multicultural marketing in this country.

She also sees a future in which the need for experts and entrepreneurs who can understand and can market to this multicultural consumer will not go away but will actually grow.

For those Latino entrepreneurs reading this book, I want you to recognize the huge market opportunity you have in front of you that you are uniquely suited to capitalize on!

You know your people better than anybody; you have been blessed with a rich cultural heritage, a deep sensibility, and a tremendous work ethic.

Many times, we see the opportunity in front of us but we don't take it. We don't take it because we might think we are not good enough or it is not for us. The model of success in this country doesn't look like us most of the time. Yet what we have to offer is needed and is wanted by many. You can see it everywhere in the US across product and service categories.

Creativity is at a premium in every single industry. We (Latinos and Latinas) have the advantage of having one foot in the Hispanic world and one in the Anglo world. We can put the dots together and come up with never thought of before ideas because of our blend of cultures. We can bring the best of our Latino heritage and the best of what we see in the US with our fresh eyes.

As I mentioned before, Latino culture offers some of the most fascinating, beautiful and flavorful inspiration in the world. It is also having a tremendous influence on mainstream America, which is adopting Latin-inspired food, music, products, and culture at a rapid rate.

Across industries, companies are investing billions to persuade us to buy their products and services. We have an immense buying power of $1.5 trillion, and our culture is creating huge business opportunities for new products and services.

So shouldn't the Latino community be the main beneficiary of these tremendous business opportunities that we are creating in this country?

Of course we should!!

Let's do our part to help our Latino community achieve their American Dreams and help them capitalize on the amazing business opportunities we are creating for ourselves.

Who better to take advantage of the huge business opportunities being created by our presence in the US than you?

Action Steps

- ✓ Realize that being a consumer doesn't build your dream but somebody else's dream
- ✓ Create something of value
- ✓ Capitalize on the Latino market opportunity

The Paths

James Altucher, the author of the best selling *Choose Yourself* book, is one of my favorite people. He writes about a near future in which there will be entrepreneurs and the freelancers who work for them. In his book, he explains why a job in today's world will not help you achieve financial freedom and fulfillment.

He goes on to explain why depending on a job in today's world is downright dangerous. The downsizing trends in the economy will only accelerate as companies look to become more efficient by outsourcing everything but its core.

In the last 18 years living in this country, I have seen how the illusion of job security has disappeared. I know very few people who have worked as an employee for a while who have not been laid off, downsized, or fired.

It happens to everybody. Companies nowadays are faced with constant pressure to cut costs, outsource and become more efficient, so if you get caught in one of these, you will get the ax. It does not matter how well you perform or how long you have worked in the company; you will be downsized if your job is not seen as necessary anymore.

In my father's generation, it used to make sense to be an employee for most of your working life because you would be well rewarded for your loyalty with a stable income during your working years and a secure retirement.

So even if you didn't like your job, for some it might have made sense to trade off work-related fulfillment for the safety it offered. You would most likely not be downsized if you did a good job, you would benefit from a steady income and benefits throughout your lifetime, and you would get a pension you could retire on.

My grandfather on my mother's side actually took that route. He always wanted to become a doctor but had to abandon his plans because he had to support his family. Instead, he worked as an accountant for all of his working years at the company owned by his brothers-in-law. He made the tradeoff to sacrifice his career dreams for a stable income to feed his family.

He passed away when I was 10 years old but in the time I was fortunate enough to spend with him, I always noticed that there was a side of him bottled up inside that he repressed. He was the kindest man I ever met, and I am sure he would have been a fantastic doctor who would have helped

157

thousands of people lead better lives. He denied the world of his gifts because he felt he had to, but you don't.
Today, the rewards for sticking it out in a job for all your working life have disappeared. Not only has job security disappeared, but pensions also don't exist anymore in the private sector. You are on your own to save for retirement, and benefits are much worse, assuming you can get them.

Aside from the lack of security, there is also a lack of upside in being an employee your entire career. The chances of climbing up the ladder all the way to the top where you could build serious wealth are pretty slim.

To top it off, a 2014 Gallup's State of the American Workplace study[4] shows that 70 percent of Americans are disengaged from their jobs. In other words, 70 percent of Americans flat-out don't like their jobs.

So aside from the lack of job security and lack of financial upside, most people are not being fulfilled by being an employee.

What all this means is that being an employee has become a low upside/high risk/low fulfillment proposition. So why would you want to devote your life to being an employee?

Employees will be laid off in the millions and will face a world in which they'll need to sell their services to the companies that fired them, for less money and without benefits. Or they'll need to become entrepreneurs.

The problem is that most of these people will not be prepared for the new work jungle. They will not be prepared because most didn't have to hone their entrepreneurial skills, lifelong learning and creativity in their jobs. Unfortunately, these are the skills that will be required to survive in the new world of work.

The new world of work, James Altucher explains, will be dominated by the creative entrepreneurs who come up with the businesses that solve the biggest problems in people's lives in the future.

They will hire low-cost freelancers to outsource their non-core work. They will create most of the value in the economy, and as a result will reap most of the rewards. The successful entrepreneurs will lead the life of their dreams. Most of the people who will work for them will probably find it much harder to make enough money or have enough time to do the same.

This is not to say it doesn't pay to be an employee while you learn your craft; after all, you will be getting paid to learn. But at some point for most people, the marginal returns of being an employee disappear and you will need to branch out on your own either full time or on the side if you want to capitalize on your full potential.

So do you want to be an entrepreneur or be the freelancer who works for them?

If you are reading this book and are passionate and serious about living the life you dream about, then you probably answered entrepreneur.

There are many different types of entrepreneurs, different levels of entrepreneurship, and a number of paths to prepare to become an entrepreneur. To prepare for the new world of work, let's explore the different types of entrepreneurial paths that are and will be available to you:

The Mediapreneur Path

"There is not a moment in the history of humanity in which it has been better, easier and more convenient to publish your own content than at this moment. People that lived in other generations depended on newspapers publishing their articles or a TV channel airing their story and if they didn't nobody would hear about them. Now the gatekeepers have disappeared."
- Gaby Natale, President, Super Latina TV

We live in a world in which technology has destroyed the barriers to building a media platform and removed its gatekeepers. The rise of blogging, You Tubing, podcasting, Vining, and online education is the result of this seismic change. This revolution has created tremendous business opportunities for entrepreneurs.

Millions of people have built their own platforms and are making a living as podcasters, bloggers, authors, speakers, You Tube personalities, etc. Some are doing it full-time and some are participating on the side.

These entrepreneurs usually work on their own, doing highly creative work, addressing important problems, and creating value for the people who follow them. They leverage technology to scale themselves, to build their audience and to create content, products and services for them. They educate, inspire and serve.

They operate in a number of industries, including education, online business, art, design, health and wellness, technology, etc.

I have interviewed many of these types of entrepreneurs in the podcast: people like Mr. Solopreneur Hour himself

160

Michael O'Neal, Ray Collazo of Latino Talk and Ray's Podcast Network, Lizza Monet Morales of XOXO, Cynthia Sanchez of Ohsopinteresting, and Jorge Narvaez of Reality Changers, among others.

Jorge Narvaez is the most famous single dad on YouTube. He started his "Reality Changers" platform to dedicate songs to his daughters. Little did he know that his "Reality Changers" channel would grow to more than 178 million visits, becoming one of the most popular Hispanic channels on You Tube in the US.

Jorge has become one of the top Hispanic You Tube stars because he is authentic; he truly cares about helping people and has a message that resonates strongly with his audience:

"Be positive, be strong and be with your family"

- Jorge Narvaez, single dad and YouTube star

His authenticity, good intentions, and message come across clearly in his videos, and his fans love him for it.

What all of these people like Jorge have in common is that they have built an audience around their platform, and that platform follows them. They provide significant amount of value to their audience in the form of free content, paid courses, or entertainment. They are known, liked and trusted by their audience because of who they are and what they do for them.

Nely Galan is the founder of the Adelante Movement and former president of Telemundo. She started off as a journalist and then became an entrepreneur in the media business. After her entrepreneurial journey, she was able to become the president of Telemundo, where she was the first woman president of a network here in the United States.

After running Telemundo very successfully for a number of years, she founded the Adelante movement, which empowers Latinas to achieve their success. She helps them through training seminars, teaching them to understand how to build their own businesses and lead successful lives. Nely has built a powerful platform for herself and is an inspiration and an example on how to build yours.

In the old days, politicians used to stand up on physical platforms to deliver their speeches. Today, the meaning of the word platform has expanded. The platform is an expression of you, your brand, and your mission. It is very powerful because it is the vehicle by which you can fulfill your calling, make a lot of money, help a lot of people, and be seen as an expert in your field, whatever that may be.

Your platform can live in all the touch points that bring it to life, such as your website, your blog, your podcast, videos, your book, trainings, events, when you give a talk, etc. The platform is the vehicle and your message in action.

With the tools we now have at our disposal, it is very easy and cheap to build your platform. But first you need to identify your mission, that problem you deeply desire to solve, and how you are going to contribute to other people's lives.

Then, build a branded platform around your mission, offering value to people through different media vehicles I have talked about. Building a platform can make you very successful as it can be a huge differentiator for you and a huge boost for your career. A platform also allows you to have a lot of impact in other people's lives.

So seriously consider building your platform. You might be asking how to go about starting one. Well, next I'll show you how I built my platform and how I continue to grow it.

How to Build a Platform

The easiest way to show you how to build a platform is by sharing my story on how I started the Logra Tu Dream platform.

As I mentioned before in this book, I realized that my mission is to do my part in helping other Latinos achieve their dreams—their dreams of securing a better future for their families and growing their entrepreneurial businesses by giving a voice to the stories of Latino & Latina role models

To inspire, mentor & provide business advice... To show that _Si Se Puede_

I wanted to write a book but never got around to it (until now). But I had a mission: I knew who I passionately wanted to help, what big problem I could help them solve, and I had an idea of how to solve the problem

Then in 2012 I discovered podcasting!

Podcasting had a profound impact in my life.

I experienced the transformative impact of podcasting. I believe podcasts have the power to change people's lives.

Podcasts are so impactful because of the storytelling and intimacy that you get from listening to stories. You can learn from and be inspired by people you like and trust.

There is something about being in somebody's ear for an hour that creates much deeper relationships.

I found Entrepreneur on Fire and was incredibly inspired by John and the stories of his guests: top entrepreneurs who have overcome failures to achieve fantastic success.

Very quickly, I became a podcast junkie. What hooked me on podcasts were the incredible stories I learned from, and the fact that they were real, relevant, and incredibly valuable to my life.

No fakeness, no scripts, and no agendas; just compelling, authentic stories from people who wanted to help me and many others.

I learned about other great podcasts like the Solopreneur Hour by Michael O'Neal, Jaime Tardy's Eventual Millionaire, and Patt Flynn's Smart Passive Income, among others.

The more I listened, the more I wanted to learn about how to become a successful entrepreneur: how to podcast, how to do great online marketing, and how to build wealth.

It was like getting another mini-MBA but better as podcasting was much more inspiring, engaging, and actionable for today's world. Because learning through stories engaged my mind and my heart.

I liked these podcasters and trusted them. I felt like I knew them.

After all, they were changing my life for the better and pushing me to reach for my dream.

I realized that podcasting was the perfect medium to tell the stories of successful Latinos and Latinas and accomplish my own mission.

At that point, the idea of *Logra Tu Dream* was born and I decided to take action.

But I had no idea how to start a podcast. I had been listening to John Lee Dumas and I learned about the power of masterminds to achieve success.

I knew he had a mastermind group, Fire Nation Elite, so I decided to give it a shot and wrote him an email asking to join his group. He replied within five minutes and we talked the next day.

In the space of a day, I found a group that helped me start my podcast. It was the best decision I made.

I committed to other 100 generous and successful entrepreneurs that I would launch in three months.

I learned from this group how to do it and, more importantly, that I *could* do it, as I saw many of them launching their podcasts successfully. I can't stress enough how important it is to have a group coaching you, supporting you, and cheering you on along the way.

I was exposed to all the best practices, and also I worked incredibly hard not to let them down. In three months and two weeks, I launched my podcast.

It's NOT hard to start a podcast (if you don't go it alone) BUT IT IS HARD WORK.

One of the most important insights I have to share with you in this book is to build a platform, not just a podcast.

In today's world, a branded platform is a powerful idea that can deliver value to your target in different mediums, products and services, and in a way that is differentiated and own-able.

It is scalable, very powerful, and monetize-able in a number of ways.

So, think branded platform, not just podcast, and maximize your potential.

As I mentioned before, you need a mission, a powerful idea to accomplish it, and a clear and discrete target that you passionately want to help.

My idea was very clear from the start: I wanted to help Latinos achieve their dream.

My target audience was very clear, too. It was Latino and Latina professionals, entrepreneurs, and students, from college-age to mid-career age who had an American Dream they were pursuing or wanted to pursue, but who were lacking mentorship, inspiration and business advice from Latino role models who could show them that it is possible.

The brand idea and target would be the heart and guiding light for my brand. First, I brainstormed for a name that

166

would bring this concept to life in a compelling, relevant way with my target audience.

I decided to choose a name in Spanglish. I came up with the simplest expression of what I wanted to achieve: "Logra Tu Dream" which means "achieve your dream" in English.

I chose this because it is a call to action to Latinos and Latinas to achieve their dreams, and because the Spanglish would connect very powerfully. I was deliberate about having the word dream be in English, as the dream is an American Dream and the Logra Tu (achieve your) in Spanish, as this represented our Latino roots and drive.

I rushed to get the urls and then all of a sudden, I was on my way to making Logra Tu Dream happen. Then I also filed a trademark on the brand to protect it.

Design (Logo and Website)

Once I had a name that I loved, I started thinking about the logo and the design. I love my Marketealo logo, as it looks like a colorful waveform that represents the passion, diversity, colors and flavors of Latino culture. So I knew I wanted to use it, if only I could find a way to fit my brand idea.

That is when I enlisted Angelina Villanueva, a brilliant Latina graphic designer.

I gave her the challenge of integrating the Marketealo wave with the Logra Tu Dream concept. She came back with a number of options, one of which I fell in love with:

Simple, elegant, powerful, and on brand. Just what I wanted: a logo that represents the path that Latinos and Latinas take towards pursuing their dream. A path that is full of passion, life, family, diversity, and color.

Website

I knew I wanted a very visual website, so I asked my mastermind group for recommendations and did my own research to find a Word Press theme that would be both visually impactful and customizable. Many people recommended the Genesis framework for its great performance and beautiful themes.

I went ahead with Studio Press for Word Press, and picked the Parallax theme that runs on the Genesis framework because it was very visual and different from others I have seen before.

The hard part was figuring out what plug-ins to use to create the experience I wanted, so I spent a lot of time asking knowledgeable people in my mastermind group and doing my own research. The process was painful, as I am not a technically-inclined person, but I did learn the basics of how to set up a decent, attractive, and functioning website. Check it out here: www.logratudream.com

For the website design, I wanted to bring the brand idea to life in an impactful and very visual way. I came up with the idea of doing a collage of different Latinos and Latinas at various stages of pursuing their dream, using a filter with the colors of the logo. This would represent all of the dreams that the podcast would help to reach. Norman Batts, a talented info-graphic designer I had worked with before, developed the collage.

Email List Building

The ability to build a list of your audience is the life-blood of any endeavor. I went ahead and used AWeber for the email opt-in and to automate the process to send out emails to provide content and value to my audience. It is a great solution that gives you all the email marketing capability you need for a very low monthly cost of about $19.

For the actual opt-in boxes/forms that I put on the website, I used App Sumo and Hybrid Connect, both of which offer great flexibility to build opt-in forms and slide-ins that look great and are easy to install on Word Press. I fumbled a bit at first, trying to create and install the forms, but once you get the process it is very easy.

Once you determine the branded platform, it is time to execute and start your podcast.

Determine what is the right format for your platform and for your personality.

For me, it was 30- 60 min interviews with successful Latino/Latin-inspired entrepreneurs and leaders, along with some solo shows.

I defined the interview structure to ensure that guests would be able to share how they had achieved their dreams through their stories, their struggles, their successes, and what they had learned.

Next, you need to figure out your set up:

I decided to go the do-it-yourself, low-cost route. The group was helping me, but I decided to do it myself vs. hiring people to do it for me so that I could master it.

You don't have to spend thousands of dollars to create a high-quality podcast; I spent $240 bucks to start off. What matters most are the platform and your passion.

First thing you need is a microphone and a laptop. I started with a $25 headset that provided good enough sound quality, and my old laptop.

I needed to record the interviews so I opted for Pamela recording software for $29. This software easily integrates with Skype, which is how I do the audio-only interviews. Now I was able to start doing the interviews.

My DIY $240.73 Podcast Startup Setup

Equipment

Logitech Headset: $24.99
Current Laptop: $0

Recording

Recording Software:
$29.78

Music

Royalty free music:
$25

Editing & Tagging

Audacity

$0

Podcast Hosting

$15/month

Website/Blog

Wordpress Theme: $99.98
Hosting: $11.99/month
Domain: $14.99/yr
Email List Building: $19/month
Design: $0

Total: $240.73

To develop the intro and outro, I needed music that would fit my platform. I bought royalty free music for $25 online. Then I recorded my intro and outro myself and edited in the music.

Now I had to learn how to edit my podcasts. For editing, I used Audacity, free software you can get online. I learned how to edit through tutorials on my mastermind group and through YouTube videos. At first it took me 4 hours to edit out all my mmms and estes, but with practice I got better and faster.

After I edited my podcast and put in the intro and outro, I had to tag it with the episodes' information, etc. For this I used ID3, which is free.

Then once you tag it, you can release it. For this, you need to host it, but not at your website hosting because if and when you build a huge audience, you will crash your website. This is why Libsyn exists; it will host your podcasts for a fee, depending on how much data you upload.

After you upload it to Libsyn, then you are ready to publish it on the different directories (iTunes, Stitcher and SoundCloud) and on your website.

To do this, you need to submit the podcast to these directories through a somewhat intricate process. Once you do this, you take the Libsyn link and publish each episode as a blog post with show notes and picture of the interviewee.

If you have done the iTunes and Stitcher set up correctly, then the podcasts will show up in the directories after you publish on your blog. The first time you publish it will take a day or two for them to show up, but after that it is almost automatic.

I recorded close to 20 interviews before I launched.

When you launch, do it with at least 4 episodes. As you will see next, it will help you to turbo boost your podcast.

The most important directory you need to succeed in by far is iTunes. You'll find 75 percent of podcast listeners there.

Then Stitcher and SoundCloud.

You need to share your podcast as much as possible to build an audience.

172

For me, Twitter, Facebook groups, and my guests and their audience were the most effective means of sharing. The beauty of having influential great people on your podcast is that not only do you get to build a relationship with them, but you also learn from them, and they bring their audience along with them.

As you build your audience, you need to build your list. If you don't have an email list, you will not be able to turn your podcast into a business. It is *that* important.

A list allows you to continue to build the relationship with your audience by providing them more value and at some point offering them your products or services.

I talked about the importance of iTunes: It is critical that you start off with a bang on iTunes.

The way to do this is to get on their New & Noteworthy (N&N) list, which can be found in the Favorite section on the podcast app. This features the top 100 New & Noteworthy podcasts across categories.

This means that you'll be right next to the top-ranking podcast lists.

This is big because people discover podcasts. Guess how they do it?

You guessed it—they browse through these lists first.

If you get enough great ratings, reviews and downloads, you get on the New & Noteworthy list on iTunes for 80 days, right out of the gate.

173

I contacted my friends, my family, and my mastermind colleagues and asked them to leave me a great review and rating if they liked the podcast. It worked; I was on the N&N list for 80 days on the Business, Career, Health and Self Help categories.

I even made it to number four in the N&N list in the career section, which put me on the front page of iTunes. This early momentum allowed me to build my audience quickly, increase my downloads, gain credibility, and attract great guests and media attention.

From there the podcast flourished, reaching thousands of people in more than 40 countries.

Shortly after I launched I hit the #4 spot in careers in New & Noteworthy in iTunes

The podcast has brought many blessings to my life. I have been able to interview and build relationships with some of the most successful people in the Latino and non-Latino world. The podcast has inspired many people to rekindle their dreams.

It has shown them that it is possible for Latinos and Latinas to achieve their success, despite any obstacles. I have also established myself as a thought leader and expert when it comes to Latino success, content creation, and podcasting.

It is a great start, but only a great start. Was it fun? You bet; it is one of the most exciting, challenging yet rewarding things I have done in my professional life.

I learned so much from doing the podcast that I felt compelled to synthesize and share this knowledge with you in this book.

I have learned that for any podcast to be successful you need to:

1. Do it with quality (provide VALUE)
2. Be consistent
3. Give to your community

The podcasting community is a giving community, much like the Hispanicize community. If you give and help others along the way, you'll get help. Other influencers will promote your platform if you promote theirs.

You'll build crucial relationships that will provide you access to incredible opportunities you never dreamed off. You will build your brand.

But if you take, you'll fail, because people don't like to help takers.

So "Give and you'll receive."

Many of you might be saying, "This is great, but what about making money?"

To illustrate the potential of the monetized podcast platform, I give you exhibit A: Entrepreneur on Fire from my friend John Lee Dumas.

John is probably one of the most successful podcasters monetizing his platform. He is on his way to making $3 million this year.

He built a platform, listened to what his audience needed, created the membership training groups Podcasters Paradise and Webinar on Fire, and the Fire Nation Elite mastermind. He also has sponsors for his podcasts, has written a book, benefits from affiliate sales, and offers coaching & group coaching.

John is one of the most generous guys out there and he is showing the world this by delivering value to his audience in the form of solutions to their biggest problems. He is proof that you can make a lot of money with podcasts.

I have chosen not to monetize yet, but I will.

So what impact has Podcasting had on my life?

The most important thing podcasting has done for me is that it has given me the ability to inspire and help many people.

Emails from listeners sharing how the podcast has inspired them to follow their dreams, and how they have seen that "si se puede" (it is possible) make all the hard work and time I put into the podcast worth it.

I have built relationships with some of the most successful Latinos & Latinas in the country, and some non-Latinos like Gary Vaynerchuk.

I have learned from them, which helped me tremendously in my own development.

I am building a brand, attracting the attention of traditional media, bloggers and podcasters. All this attention has helped me increase my reach even more.

What's Next?

I wrote and published this book, which will take the mission of Logra Tu Dream to the next level.

This book would not have been possible without the podcast. I am extending the branded platform and this is only the start.

Steps To Build Your Platform

1. Have a Mission (YOUR WHY)
2. Define who you passionately want to help
3. Build a platform, NOT just a podcast
4. Solve one of your target's biggest problems
5. Don't go it alone; start with the support of a community
6. Leverage proven best practices
7. Give back!!

The Tech Startup Entrepreneur Path

There are tremendous opportunities in building new tech-based businesses that solve big problems. In the last 18 years since I've lived in the US, I have seen how new startups disrupt almost every industry, growing into multi-billion dollar corporations: from Google to Amazon, Facebook to AirBnB, to countless others.

Technology keeps advancing as the costs for starting a business that might disrupt an industry keep decreasing. Now anyone can truly aspire to create the next startup that will revolutionize an industry.

Peter Diamandis the founder of the X-Prize, entrepreneur and author of *Bold* is without a doubt one of the most extraordinary visionaries of our time. In his book *Bold*, he talks about what he sees as the biggest business opportunities which will produce the next group of billionaires: robotics, infinite computing, synthetic biology, artificial intelligence, networks and sensors technologies. Peter also makes the point that you don't need to be a technologist to play this game. These are opportunities ripe for the most ambitious entrepreneurs to pursue.

But it is not an easy path...

Startups are not as glamorous as you might think. It is easy to want to be that guy on the cover of Fast Company who built his startup to become the latest billion dollar, industry-changing business. But in reality, startups are very tough. As Pablo Fuentes and Jesse Martinez put it, there is nothing glamorous about startups.

Expect to work very long hours for little or no pay, with high levels of stress knowing that there is a very good chance your startup will fail. This is not to discourage anyone from trying to build their next startup but to set the expectations of what you may get into if you decide to take this route.

However, there is a way to lower the risk of starting up a tech business. It is the Lean Startup methodology. This methodology calls for the entrepreneur to validate his startup business idea at a smaller scale before going all in and investing significant amounts of time and money in a business.

This is how it works:

✓ Entrepreneurs build a minimal viable product (like its name says, it is a very rough expression of what your product can be)
✓ Then they test it out in the market at a small scale to get feedback on whether people will actually buy the product and if it solves their problem.
✓ They also get feedback as to what works, what doesn't, and how to improve it.
✓ With the feedback in hand the entrepreneur improves the product, getting even more market feedback until they get to a product they know has strong demand and that solves the customers' problem it was meant to solve.

Pablo Fuentes, whom I interviewed in episode three of the Logra Tu Dream podcast, advocates for the Cross 10 method. This approach helps entrepreneurs validate whether people would buy a product or service without having to build a product. All it takes is setting up a landing page, announcing your product where people can "buy" it.

Once people click to buy, a screen appears, informing them that it is just a test and that you'll let them know if and when you launch it. Pablo says that if you can't get 10 people to buy your product, you don't have an idea that merits putting any further effort into it, so you need to go back to the drawing board.

This approach is a simple and effective way to save yourself a lot of time, money and pain trying to build something people won't buy.

There are tremendous opportunities in the Latino market waiting for you to seize. I encourage you to take this path if

179

you have a strong desire to change the world, if you are willing to work very hard, and if you can stomach the risk.

But if you do, I highly recommend you validate your idea first so that you don't have to experience the unnecessary pain I experienced when I failed to build itradefood.com into a successful business back in 1999/2000.

I failed because I didn't validate my idea. Instead, I invested two years of my life, a good portion without pay. I worked extremely hard trying to build a business that was just too early for its time.

I was able to raise money, I hired a small team, and I put in my best efforts to try to make it happen. But only a few customers were willing to take a chance at putting their supply chains online back when the Internet was in its infancy.

Had somebody like Pablo advised me before I took the plunge, I would have learned that there was not a business there and I would have done something else, saving myself a lot of time, pain, and money.

I learned a tremendous amount about business and about myself throughout this experience, but I wish I could have learned the same with less pain. As Warren Buffett says, *"You learn by mistakes, but they don't have to be yours."*

This is not to say to be afraid. On the contrary, if you have a deep desire to solve a given problem and the inclination to go all in, go ahead and start your venture NOW.

You need to listen to your gut. Just be sure to validate your idea before you invest significant time and money. If you fail, fail fast, and either pivot or change direction. But whatever you do, keep moving forward.

The Latino Startup Funding Challenge

Jose Huitron is founder of Crowdisimo and Hub 81, a new venture design agency; he also leads the California Central Coast chapter of the Latino Startup Alliance. He advises aspiring entrepreneurs to join the Latino Startup Alliance to be able to meet potential investors and other entrepreneurs, and to gain access to Silicon Valley.

We are the new minority majority; we represent a massive $1.5 trillion in spending power and we are improving our incomes. We have entrepreneurship in our DNA and some in our community are plunging into the startup waters.

Entrepreneurs like Pablo Fuentes, Edrizio de la Cruz, Komal Dadlani, Camilo Anabalon, and Felix Ortiz III, all of whom I have interviewed on the Logra Tu Dream podcast, have started their companies successfully and raised capital through hard work, dedication and hustle.

They are proof that it is possible but not easy to raise capital for your venture. Aside from their incredible dedication, hard work and hustle, these entrepreneurs have started companies that solve important problems that people care about and are willing to pay for:

- ✓ Pablo Fuentes started Proven, a leading hospitality industry hiring tool. Proven makes hiring processes seamless for restaurants and hotels on both mobile and desktop.

- ✓ Edrizio de La Cruz started Regalii, a company that allows immigrants to use their mobile devices to track and pay bills for family in Latin America.

✓ Komal Dadlani started Lab4U, a platform that enables hands-on lab experiences through web and mobile devices, delivering low-cost solutions for science education.

✓ Camilo Anabalon started Babybe, a company that keeps mothers and pre-term babies connected through the process of artificial incubation through an innovative bionic mattress.

But yet, when was the last time you read about a super successful Latino startup on Tech Crunch?

In my interview with Jose Huitron, he talked about the lack of access to capital for Latino entrepreneurs. Only 1 to 2 percent of venture capital goes to Latino and African American entrepreneurs.

We have very limited access to venture capital. We don't have "the rich uncle" or access to the exclusive networks of venture capital investors, most of which are not Latino.

There is a lack of education about the startup opportunities in the Latino market among investors. I found this out first hand when I helped the Multicultural venture accelerator Nuevo Labs.

The lack of access to investors and lack of familiarity with Latino startup opportunities result in very few Latino startups getting funded. This lowers the probability of Latino startups succeeding, which in turn results in a lack of Latino startup success stories that can increase investor interest in funding Latino startups.

It is a vicious cycle that needs to be broken. This is why the work that Jose Huitron, Jesse Martinez, and Deldelp Medina are doing at the Latino Startup Alliance and at Avion Ventures is so critically important. They are building a bridge between Latino entrepreneurs and Silicon Valley investors and other entrepreneurs. They are connecting them to the sources of potential capital and resources they need to make their ventures successful.

The Corporate Path

"The more you can be part of them, the easier the transition will be"
- David Gomez, President & CEO of David Gomez and Associates.

David Gomez is the President & CEO of David Gomez and Associates. He has built a very successful career in the executive search business, focusing on Hispanic talent.

David has a lifetime of experience placing Latinos in corporate America from middle management to the highest levels. Despite great advances, he still sees that corporate America is still celebrating their culture and not ours.

He advises all Latino candidates to do their due diligence and really understand how diverse the company's work force they are interviewing with really is. He asks them to make sure they know what their track record is with Latino employees so that they understand what they are getting into and so they can avoid potential career disasters.

David has realized that for Latinos to be successful in corporate America at the highest level, they need to "do in Rome as Romans do," adapting to meet companies halfway as companies will not be adapting to them. Latinos also need to work harder than anyone else and never give up.

David's call to all of us is to unite hand in hand and help each other out. When he prepares candidates for interviews, he tells them:

"When you go into that interview, I want you to get hired. If you do get hired, don't forget me; put your hand behind your back and bring two or three others with you. Open those doors and once we unite as a Latino nation, that's when we are really going to get the great spoils of this country."

David believes that we live in one of the greatest countries in the history of the world at the right time. He sees a world filled with opportunities, and he urges us to think about doing the hard work, trusting in God, and then watching what happens. One of my key takeaways from my conversation with David was that we just need to ask for help to get ahead. People will help us if we ask.

David believes in our people's talent and generosity, and sees a bright future for us in corporate America and beyond.

How to land your dream job

Marissa Fernandez is the Director of Hispanic Fan Strategy & Marketing for the National Football League. She has what many consider to be a dream job, working for the NFL in a fun job that supports her community. Marissa has been very successful in her corporate career.

She worked hard to get into a great university, earning her bachelors' degree at Cornell University. She started her career in marketing at Procter & Gamble, the consumer products giant, and the best marketing school in the world, in my humble opinion.

From there, she was recruited to the Latinum Network; a company where she helped Fortune 500 companies develop strategies to win in the Hispanic market. At Latinum she worked with the NFL, who was one of her clients.

Then one day she was recruited by the NFL, who was looking for a director for Hispanic Fan Engagement. She had become the obvious choice for the job; she was already an expert in Hispanic marketing at the highest level with a great track record of success, helping brands at P&G and at Latinum succeed in this market. Marissa also had a relationship with the NFL, having worked with them.

She got her dream job at the NFL because she had woven and mastered her ONE "thread" that connects and combines her mission, her unique set of skills, experiences, and work. In the process, she created tremendous value around her unique skills and experience.

Marissa had gained a high level of skill in consumer brand marketing; she had deep knowledge of and experience in the Hispanic market and the "Total Market" approach, and she was actively giving back to her community. She loved sports and wanted to marry her love of sports with her brand marketing craft in a way that would serve her community.

The NFL was looking for somebody who would bring this precise value to them and Marissa was right there, in the right place at the right time...

Marissa is transforming the NFL, helping them educate and attract more Latino football fans. She has worked with the NFL's Hispanic media partners to bring the game in Spanish to more people, and in a more relevant way. She is also bringing the NFL game to Latino kids through the NFL Play60 Character Camps.

The camps help the kids get into football, inspiring them to follow their local teams. The camps are not just about football; they also instill character in kids so that they conduct themselves as good people in life and lead active healthy lifestyles.

These are only some of the projects Marissa is leading at the NFL, which are having a big impact, helping transform the most popular sport in the US by making it more accessible and attractive to Latino fans.

Marissa's credits her success to the following factors:

- **Focusing on relationships:** Her family is a source of encouragement for Marissa, who are always there for her in the good times and difficult times. She also actively invests time in her professional networks, seeking out mentors who have guided her through her career and also taking on mentees that she can help.

- **Being accountable:** Marissa always delivers or over delivers on expectations in her work. She has proven to be a very reliable person who always delivers to the companies she has worked for. This quality has allowed her to build strong personal brand equity, which has been critical to her success.

- **Have confidence in yourself**: Marissa urged the Logra Tu Dream community to not be afraid of taking risks. She believes that if you believe in yourself, you can accomplish anything.

- **Keeping a balance:** *"My job isn't who I am; that is not what defines me,"* Marissa says. Spending enough quality time with her family, giving back to her community, and staying in shape keep things in perspective and keep her balanced. Achieving balance

186

in our lives is critical to success in our work; if we are
not in balance, we burn out.

Marissa demonstrates that it is possible to find your
fulfillment and maximize your potential in corporate
America but it is getting increasingly difficult to do so. In
order to succeed at the highest levels, doing work you love
and that fulfills you in corporate America, you need to be
incredibly talented and hardworking, and you need to master
your ONE thread. You need to deliver your unique value to
the companies that need it in spades, just like Marissa does.

You also need to be smart about managing your career so
that, more often than not, you can be in the right place at the
right time. You will need to be comfortable dealing with
corporate politics, bureaucracy, and some of the nonsensical
things that tend to happen in these environments. You will
need to learn how to navigate these large organizations
effectively to become successful.

In my experience in corporate America, I found that it is not
enough to excel at your job. You need to learn how to
conduct yourself in a way that helps you attract allies and
neutralize detractors.

You need to learn how to manage your boss and your boss'
boss so that your work is presented in the best way possible
to the higher-ups. They will either become a fan of yours,
ignore you, or want you out of there.

Unlike entrepreneurs, corporate professionals need to
become great organizational navigators to be able to survive
and thrive. If navigating comes naturally to you, then the
corporate world is for you. If not, I suggest you do not waste
your time and instead focus on paths that will provide you a
higher probability of success.

Sandra Alfaro's Multicultural Marketing Path to Success

"My American Dream is to be able to raise my son to be equally comfortable in both worlds. I want him to love the flavors, the sounds, the customs, and the traditions of Peru and the Caribbean, and at the same time I want him to feel the pride that I feel in being American. I want to be able to provide him the opportunity for a great education, security and a future but really to make sure he is living both worlds because that is truly a blessing."

– Sandra Alfaro, Managing Partner, Wing Agency

Sandra Alfaro is the Managing Partner of Wing, one of the nation's top multicultural marketing agencies. She has dedicated 20 years of her life to mastering the craft of multicultural marketing. Sandra has helped some of the biggest brands in the country win in the Latino and multicultural market.

She worked at a number of top agencies such as Saatchi & Saatchi, The Vidal Partnership, Lopez Negrete Communications, and is now rising to the top of her field at Wing.

Growing up, she was aware that her parents made a lot of sacrifices to be in this country, being away from their families. Back then it was much harder for Latinos to make it, so she was very aware of that sacrifice. Sandra knew her parents had sacrificed so much so that she could have a better education that would lead to better opportunities in her life. Her education has always been at the core of her successful journey.

Sandra realized early on the huge, competitive advantage that her ability to speak Spanish represented in her career prospects. She started her career at Saatchi & Saatchi, working for Conill Advertising, their Latino market subsidiary.

Sandra landed in exactly the right career opportunity for her skill set: multicultural marketing. Being in the right stream allowed her to become one of the top multicultural marketing executives in the country.

After education, she considers curiosity as her next most important success factor, as it has fueled her desire to continue learning. As I mentioned earlier in the book, the desire to continue to learn is critical to be able to constantly adapt and succeed in today's world and in the future.

Sandra is a big believer in fostering an environment of mentoring; she has had several mentoring relationships over the years that have helped her advance in her career. The mentors have provided important feedback to help her improve and have offered a safe place to go for career advice.

Sandra's advice to young Latino marketers is to be a "Hispanic Professional" not a "Professional Hispanic." This means that Latinos wanting to pursue a career in marketing should contribute to the overall business and not just to the Latino market piece. This is very important because otherwise you can get pigeon-holed to only Latino market related roles.

She urges young Latino marketers to see themselves as marketers who happen to have this Latino market expertise that adds to their arsenal of marketing skills.

If you are a Latino/a working in marketing, capitalize on the edge you will have in the Latino market but also get experience and become proficient in general market roles. This will give you an even bigger edge as you will be able to do both Latino and general market work and can easily jump from one world to the other.

To maximize your potential not only as a marketer but in any field, you need to be able to transform your bicultural background and bilingual ability into a competitive advantage in the workplace.

One of the most beautiful realizations I have had since I started the Logra Tu Dream podcast is that today, being Latino or Latina in the US is no longer a disadvantage. It is actually a big advantage if you know how to harness it...

The Artistic Path

"Listen to what you really like to do. When you are very young you tend to think you really have to study a certain degree because people think that is the way to go. The best way is to just listen to your heart and to what your true interests are. We don't need to give in to the pressures of the outside world."

- Kyra Caruso, DJ and Doula

Aside from interviewing successful Latino entrepreneurs, community leaders, authors, marketers and executives, I have also interviewed artists on the Logra Tu Dream podcast. These artists demonstrate that success can be found in any field, even in art, which is a field many consider to be one that is nearly impossible to make a living.

Kyra Caruso is a Latina/New York native with a very interesting mix of professions: she is a DJ and a doula. Part Mexican and part Austrian, Kyra is co-owner of the music and lifestyle company, Blend Media Group. Caruso has

become quite the hot commodity, even DJing for the likes of Katy Perry and Rihanna.
If playing music for celebrities isn't enough, Kyra is a certified doula, and is especially passionate about meeting the needs of immigrant, single and low-income women in her community. Through her work as a doula, Kyra launched a program called Beyond Words: music therapy for mothers and their babies during labor.

Kyra landed DJ gigs with big celebrities by promoting parties for many years and by playing good music that touched people at an emotional level. Celebrities went to her parties and got exposed to her music; they were touched by her music, which got her invited to DJ at private celebrity parties. She was consistent and patient in her work and credits her success to networking, persistence, and to avoiding envy of other successful people.

She found that by congratulating other people on their successes, success would come back to her. She believes that this happens because she was planting good karma by helping people and showing good will. As a doula, she has taken clients who could not afford her, and when DJing she would teach up and coming DJs, bringing them along to her gigs.

Erick "ROHO" Garcia is an up and coming Latino artist, DJ and soccer player. A Chicago native raised in Joliet, Illinois, he is now completing his master's degree, studying painting.

Erick shows us why you don't have to be a "starving artist" if you choose a creative artist career. Through hustle, he has found success as an artist. He has learned that to be a successful artist, it is more important to hustle than to be the most talented. He has seen many artists more talented than him fail because they don't have the hustle in them like he does.

Through hustle, Erick has landed big exhibitions in his hometown of Chicago, which has given his work much exposure. He believes in just getting out there, making connections. He has no problem asking for help and creating opportunities that can help him gain more exposure.

"Many times fulfillment in life is not the search for the material but it is the search of your personal path, and this path in my case was painting, which opened a very interesting and intimate world of plastic expression and other visual sensibility which I had not experienced before. Painting has also helped me to have more and better friends with which I have deeper human communication with. Painting spurred my love of reading and reading has in turn inspired my painting."

- Esteban Arias, abstract expressionist painter

Esteban Arias Murueta is an abstract expressionist painter; he changed careers in his forties, from architect to painter. He did it because he had always been an artist deep inside, and because his children had finally finished school so he was able to take on this lower paying career.

Esteban has flourished as an artist, becoming one of the best expressionist painters in Mexico, having exhibited in Mexico and the US. Most importantly, he has crafted the life he wants; he wakes up each morning, taking his walks in the beautiful "Los Viveros" park in the historic Coyoacan neighborhood in Mexico City.

Then he walks over to his favorite coffee shop, El Jarocho, and has breakfast. He then goes to work in his studio. In the evenings and on the weekends, he shares good times with his many friends at the sports club he attends and at other

Esteban has no schedule and leads a life many would envy. He is already in his seventies but he sports very few gray hairs. He has lived life to the fullest, doing what he loves, and that, my friends, is what it is all about.

If your heart tells you to be an artist, you should pursue your art with passion. Don't give in to outside influences that push you to conform and to take a "real job" or study something that is "useful." If creating great art is your mission, you need to pursue it, as this is how you will find your success.

The Side Hustle Path

Today you'll find increasingly that many people have what I call a side hustle. A side hustle is an entrepreneurial activity you can do while you have a job.

So why should you consider side hustling?

As I mentioned earlier, there is no such thing as job security any more. Today just having a job is a very risky proposition. You might feel that you are safe and you might be making a very good living...

But if you are not developing your entrepreneurial muscle and you are not working towards your mission, you are in harm's way.

It is very likely that, through no fault of your own, at some point in your career you will lose your job and be forced to become an entrepreneur, whether that means being a freelancer or owning a small business. But you will not be prepared for the new work jungle and you will struggle to make a good living if you don't make a conscious effort to build your entrepreneurial muscle by hustling on the side.

You might also miss a big opportunity to prosper like you haven't prospered before. You might miss the opportunity to build a business around your life and gain the time freedom you desire.

We live in a time in which we have the tools to build a significant business with very little investment. We can work from anywhere and set up automated systems that help leverage ourselves to serve many people without too much of our time.

This is why many people are side hustling. They realize they need to get ready for the new world of work, and they want to pursue their mission and work on their own terms. So they are taking the plunge, but on the side, managing their risk and conserving their income while they learn, explore and hone their entrepreneurial muscle.

A number of the Latinos and Latinas I interviewed on Logra Tu Dream are successfully side hustling.

Ray Collazo is the founder of Ray's Podcast Network. He started as the host of the Latino Talk podcast and then also created the Latino Sports Talk podcast. Ray is not only an accomplished podcaster, but he is also leading the political affairs for a prominent national civil rights organization serving the Latino community. Ray has a great job while doing his podcast network on the side.

He makes a good stable income from his day job and is building his dream at the same time. By focusing both his job and his podcasting venture in the Latino community, he is able to build his expertise, network and personal brand faster and more effectively. What he does and whom he meets in his job helps him with his podcast network and vice versa.

He followed his calling to help empower people and to help them realize that they are the boss of their own life. Ray has seen how Latino families encourage kids to follow the safe path, but this path is limiting our potential. This realization inspired him to transition from activist to entrepreneur.

"It's okay to have a life and to make a lot of money"
- Ray Collazo, Founder Latino Talk

Ray is working to help people generate passive income so they can have a life and make a lot of money. He knows that you need to own your content online and have your own website so that you can monetize your platform. It is very important to figure out whom you want to serve in the online world and what transferable skills you have that you can transfer to the online world to build your business.

"Regardless of what you're starting from, you can achieve greatness"
– Ray Collazo, Founder Latino Talk

Ray knows that having a job with a stable income gives him much more leeway with his podcast network venture, something he would not have if he did the podcast full time.

If he did the podcast full time, he would be pressured to make a living off of it but it might take him some time to do that. So he would have to eat through his savings or maybe even go back to work, but now having lost a portion of his savings.

On the other hand, if Ray just had his job and didn't have his podcast network side hustle, he would not be working toward his dream and would not be fulfilled. He also would not have benefited from the expanded network and expertise and the personal brand building. He wouldn't have helped

195

and entertained the thousands of people who have benefited from listening to him.

So for him, as for me, it makes sense to have a side hustle—a side hustle that gets you closer to your dream and that creates value for people.

This side hustle model has worked great for me, too, working as a Marketing Director for a company focused on the Latino community, and building the Logra Tu Dream platform by doing the podcast and now writing the book. All of these activities serve the Latino community.

My platform and day job feed on each other and complement each other. They have allowed me to go deeper into my niche (the Latino community) and have accelerated my path to becoming a well-known expert and thought leader in the Latino world.

I am building my platform and I am also improving my skill set as a Latino brand builder. The more I help people, the more I feel that I am fulfilling my mission, and the more I establish myself as an the expert in my field.

Side Hustling vs. Going All In

Many of you might be asking: How do I start side hustling and what type of side hustles can I do if I work all day and have a life?

We always have time but we just don't see that time. Just think about the time you might be spending watching TV or on other activities that might not be adding value to your life, like spending way too much time on Facebook. I have been guilty of it myself in the past.

You can cut those activities and you will find some time for your side hustle. Maybe it is just an hour or two a day. What is important is that you get started...

You should get started on a side hustle that leverages a skill you already have but that puts you in a path to where you want to go. It must be aligned with your dream and the short term goal you have set for yourself.

If you are a financial professional and your dream is to build a business around helping people to become debt free and build wealth, you might start taking on some clients whom you can coach on how to eliminate debt and build wealth. You will want to create a platform, as I mentioned previously in this book, to build your audience. You can then develop a system that you can offer in an online course to this audience and build your business.

The side hustle is a way to become an entrepreneur with lower risk versus going all-in. If you go all in as an entrepreneur, as I have done before, and you fail, you might run through your savings and then have little to nothing to fall back on.

On the other hand, if you side hustle, you will continue to have income from your job while you learn the skills and knowledge you need to make your business successful.

If your business fails, you still have an income and you can apply what you learned to another side hustle business that might be a better fit for you. If you succeed, awesome! Now you can quit your job as soon as you generate the same level of income from the side hustle that you made from your job.

Some of you might want to keep your job and stable income and your side hustle for a long while. This path might suit your current family situation better at this point in your life.

It will give you some extra income and the fulfillment of working towards your dream, even though it will take much longer to go after your dream full time.

Side Hustling to Grow your Career

Fernando Labastida is a prominent Latino business blogger and the founder of Latin IT Marketing, a blog and consultancy providing marketing services for Latin American software development firms wanting to enter the US market. Fernando is also the founder of Content Propulsion, a content marketing company for the B2B industry.

He was a pioneer in the content marketing scene, having founded the Austin Content Marketing meet up, and launching the first Spanish-language content marketing blog for the Latin American market.

He writes for the Content Marketing Institute, Relevance and AGBeat, and has spoken at SXSW and the CIES Social Media Summit in El Salvador. He has helped B2B technology companies from large to small by executing bold, content marketing initiatives.

Fernando is side hustling, as he also works as a social media manager for an Austin company.

Fernando has built deep expertise in B2B content marketing, market entry strategies for Latin IT firms trying to enter into the US market and social media. He has side hustled for a while, an approach that has worked well for him, giving him the time he needs to explore, validate and perfect different business ventures without much risk.

At the same time, he has built a great personal brand for himself, which has helped him in his businesses. He has

198

enjoyed a stable income from his job and is able to apply what he learns in his side hustle to his job.

How you can juggle a job, your platform, and freelancing

Tanya Salcido is the co-founder of Latina Geeks. She is a social media strategist and early adopter of technology who is very skilled in digital branding, online communications, and marketing.

Tanya has a day job, working for a health brand, doing social media marketing. On the side, she runs Latina Geeks and also does some freelancing.

Latina Geeks empowers Latinas to embrace technology. It is the go to content platform for Latinas on the latest news and trends in tech and social media.

With Latina Geeks, she amplifies in-store promotions for major brands through social media, getting paid and having a lot of fun at the same time. Tanya and her partner have focused on a niche that nobody was paying attention to. In the process, she has attracted many brands that sponsor her content and collaborate with her on promotions.

Tanya also freelances on social media strategy and community development on the side. When she is asked how she does it all, she responded, *"When you love something so much, you just find the time."*

I have started businesses going all-in both times. I did it taking on high risk and without validating my business before going all in or with a job to fall back on. I have realized that side hustling is a smart alternative to validate your business with much lower risk while allowing you to pursue your dreams.

Fortunately, today we have access to technology that allows us to work from anywhere. This technology also provides us the automation to start businesses that don't require that much time, that can develop once and monetize many times, and that you can do in your sleep, as you will read in the section on passive income in the next chapter.

It takes time to figure out and validate a new business. You just need some runway to take off, and side hustling provides you this runway...

Just to say thanks for buying and reading my book, I would like to give you the Audiobook version 100% FREE! Go to: www.logratudream.com/freeaudiobook

Action Steps

- ✓ Make a decision to pursue your dream.
- ✓ Realize that being a consumer doesn't build your dream but somebody else's dream.
- ✓ Create something of value.
- ✓ Look for ways you might be able to capitalize on the Latino market opportunity.
- ✓ Figure out what is the right path for you that aligns with your mission, your dreams, your existing and future skills, and your knowledge.
- ✓ Build your platform.
- ✓ Go all in or make time for side hustling (turn off the TV).
- ✓ Read this book again, focusing on the sections of surrounding yourself with the right people, getting mentored, mastering the ONE thread you can do better than anybody else, building a network, building a platform, and taking massive action.
- ✓ Take Action!

Chapter 15

COMPOUNDING

"The ability of an asset to generate earnings, which are then reinvested in order to generate their own earnings."

- Investopedia

Compounding is said to be the 8th marvel of the world. It is one of the most powerful forces in life because it turns very small gains into huge ones over time. Most people are aware of financial compounding, but compounding also applies to your career.

The work you do generates earnings, so investing in mastering your craft can have a compound effect in your career and your business. After all, as we saw in Chapter 8, "Invest in yourself to become a learning machine." You are your most valuable asset. Investing and re-investing in yourself will yield the highest returns. These returns will compound to make you incredibly wealthy if you invest in yourself.

Understanding this concept is critical because if you do, you can use it to improve your life and your finances in enormous magnitudes.

If you improve consistently in your craft, just a little every day, you will improve by orders of magnitude over the years, which will then increase your earnings. If you focus intently on mastering your craft for 10 years, as Malcolm Gladwell eloquently explains in his best-selling book, *Outliers*, you will undoubtedly become one of the top experts in your field. This is true for the simple reason that very few people do this; most people don't put in the hard work and practice that truly mastering a craft entails.

As I mentioned earlier, doing work that builds on your strengths not only leads to mastery but also brings you more happiness.

One of the key factors that differentiate the successful people from the unsuccessful is that the winners put in consistent practice. As a result, they improve consistently, benefiting from the incredible power of compounding. They build on

202

improvement upon improvement, which accelerates their rate of learning and success exponentially.

In finance, compounding is probably the most important force to build wealth because small amounts of money invested can turn into millions of dollars over time.

If you start saving only $100 a month starting at age 21 you will become a millionaire by age 66 (assuming a 10 percent yearly return on index funds). That is starting with no money and saving a relatively low amount per month.

If you make an average of $40K a year in this 45 year period which will mean you will make about ~$2,500/month after taxes, $100 will only represent 4 percent of this take home pay. It is about what I spend on my monthly smart phone bill. Is it worth it to save what you spend on your smart phone bill to retire a millionaire? I say it is very much worth it!!

It's Not What You Make, It's What You Save & Invest

If you want to be a millionaire, you don't have to earn hundreds of thousands of dollars. What you need to do is to start saving and investing as early as you can in your life. If you start saving $100 a month at age 35, it will take you until you are 80 to become a millionaire (assuming the same 10 percent yearly return) so you would have to wait 24 more years, at which point it might be too late to even matter.

As you can see, it makes a big difference to start saving and investing early. Also, you need to be able to NOT touch your investments so they can grow and benefit from compounding.

The Power of Index Funds

Tony Robbins recently wrote a book, *Money, Master the Game*, which I devoured. I devoured it because of the invaluable financial wisdom it imparted. Tony interviewed some of the best financial minds in the world, learning how they invested to make billions of dollars. Tony found that Index funds are the highest return and lower cost investment vehicles for the average person.

They are more effective because they return what the market returns and Tony shows it is practically impossible to beat the market, even for the experts, not to mention the average investor. They also have much lower costs than mutual funds, most of which have a number of hidden fees that will cut into your returns, which will then slow the compounding effect and limit your wealth building.

But before you can start investing, you need to get rid of all your debt and have an emergency fund that will provide you much needed insurance for a rainy day. And there is always a rainy day in the horizon...

"More than half of Latinos in this country don't have more than $1000 saved."

-Andres Gutierrez, Host of Paz Financiera

The state of our finances in the Latino community is very concerning, to say the least. Andres Gutierrez, the host of Paz Financiera and Dave Ramsey's Hispanic personal finance guru, puts it this way: *"If you don't take control of your finances, it will be very difficult for your dream to come true."*

Andres went from being in a deep hole of debt that was threatening his marriage to paying off all his debts and thriving financially by following Dave Ramsey's Baby Steps system, which he now teaches to the Latino community in this country.

Andres has found that there is a problem in the Latino community as it relates to getting into debt and not being able to pay it. Most of the time, it is because of a lack of information, and because we over-extend ourselves. We see our dream many times as buying a house, but this desire is so strong that it sometimes leads to bad decisions and we end up buying more house that we can afford.

We came to this country and left everything behind, working very hard to get ahead, but sometimes we don't know how to manage our finances. The outcome is that we end up like the hamster, spinning our wheels, and we don't get ahead.

Andres helps people with his 6 baby steps to financial independence. He is a big believer in self-education and in being able to turn around your financial situation in 30 days by applying the baby steps system he teaches. You need to get to a point in which you get really angry and tired of being in debt to be able to change your habits and attack your debt furiously.

The first and most important thing you need to do is to GET ON A BARE BONES WRITTEN BUDGET that you and your significant other (if you have one) commit to honoring. Then:

1. **Save $1000 for your emergency fund in the first 30 days:** To do this, you need to create a written budget in which you assign each dollar you earn to covering your costs and debts.

2. **Pay off all your debt:** Start by cutting up your credit cards. To do this, you need to realize that

getting into debt to impress others only leads to financial ruin and that you don't deserve to buy anything unless you have money to buy it. Does it make sense to pay more for things than they cost? Of course not, right? But credit cards make you do exactly that. You'll pay $120 for something worth $100 because of the interest you will end up paying. Pay your smaller debts in full, first one by one while paying minimums on the rest of the debts. Once you finish paying one, you move on to the next one and the next one until you are done.

3. **Save 3 to 6 months of living expenses for your emergency fund:** When you get to this point, you will begin to experience financial peace.

4. **Invest 15% of your income for your retirement in your 401k or IRAs:** Take advantage of your company 401K match if you have this benefit as it is free money. If you don't have your own home yet, you can save for your down payment here and then get a 15-year, fixed rate mortgage.

5. **Save for your kid's college fund:** You can save for your kids' college through 529 college savings funds or Coverdell ESAs (Education Savings Accounts).

6. **Pay off your home mortgage:** Put in any extra money you can toward the mortgage and you will save thousands of dollars of interest and months (or years) of not having a payment. If you currently have an adjustable rate mortgage, interest only, or even a 30-year mortgage, consider refinancing to a 15-year fixed-rate mortgage and pay off your home faster.

7. **Build wealth and give:** This is the last step and the one in which you get to build wealth, and be as

206

generous as you want. This is where you can leave an inheritance for your familia and leave a legacy. With no debt and no payments, you can do anything you want, all because you persevered and embraced the good habits of financial discipline that got you here.

Andres recommends that when you finish paying your debt, continue to take advantage of the habit you have formed of making payments every month. But instead of paying debt, pay yourself to build your emergency fund quickly, and then invest for retirement.

The key to Andres' approach is for you to make the decision to get out of debt and turn your financial life around.

Andres talks about three ingredients of prosperity for the Latino community:

1. **Living in the land of opportunity:** For those of us lucky enough to live in the US, the most prosperous country in the history of the world, we get the chance to start on third base as compared to very poor countries.

2. **Working hard:** We are very hard workers; it is in our nature. We have the right attitude and are not afraid of working harder than anybody else. So we have an edge as it relates to our ability to put in the hustle needed to prosper.

3. **Managing your finances well:** This has been the missing piece so far until now, as people like Andres are bringing this much-needed financial management education to our community to help them achieve financial prosperity.

This financial management component is a critical step that you need to master in order to achieve your dream. Without mastering money, you will not be able to be prosperous, and without prosperity you will not have the means to create the life you want.

To become good at managing our money is not just about learning the concepts that Andres teaches; it is about changing the way we see money in our lives. It is about choosing to invest our money in experiences over objects, recognizing that it is experiences and time spent with family and friends that bring us more happiness, not material possessions.

It is about realizing the futility of striving to keep up with other people and that our overconsumption leads us to poverty, not happiness.

Avoid Debt Like the Plague

Andres has found that debt is one of the biggest obstacles to wealth that people face.

If you get in debt to buy things you can't afford—for whatever reason—you end up having to make monthly payments, which prevent you from being able to save. If you don't save, you can't get the compound effect to work for you.

When you get in debt the compound effect works against you

Debt is like a spreading virus that, left untreated, will grow and grow, multiplying itself to a point where you can't control it. If you don't attack the debt hard, paying off big chunks of it at a time, your interest on the debt will make it grow. You will dig yourself a hole of debt payments that will be very hard to get out of.

Not only are you paying debt payments to control the ever-expanding debt, but you are also not saving when you are in debt. You are preventing yourself from benefitting from the huge benefits the compound effect can have to multiply your savings.

So the next time you want to buy something you don't have money for, STOP for a moment before you buy it with that credit card. Realize that if you buy it with a credit card, not only will you pay more than it is worth but you will also in effect be limiting your ability to build wealth and achieve your dream.

Remember: every dollar you rack up in credit card debt really costs you at least one dollar and fifteen cents (assuming the typical 15 percent interest), as you have to pay principal plus interest.

To this cost, you also need to add the cost of lost opportunity: not investing your money. In this case, let's assume your opportunity would have been to gain 10 percent in appreciation if you had invested the money in a good index fund. You would have made ten cents in one year. So in one year, that one dollar purchase really cost you $1.25. That is a 25 percent premium you are paying because you are choosing to go into debt.

Over time, if you are like most people and don't pay your credit card right away, it will cost you much more money because of compound interest. With debt, compounding works against you; it actually gets you in a much bigger debt hole than you initially thought, and it does this very quickly if you don't pay it right away.

So you end up with a bigger debt and a bigger monthly payment, which only delays the date when you can start saving, investing, and getting compounding to work for you.

Time lost not investing and compounding your money never comes back.

This is a simple example that shows that if you are serious about someday achieving financial independence, you should avoid debt at all costs. The only debt that Andres Gutierrez agrees with is the 15-year mortgage, and only when you have 3 to 6 months worth of living expenses in an emergency fund and have a 20 percent down payment saved.

Then, in step 6 of his system, he advises paying off the home mortgage as fast as you can to be totally debt free and own your home free and clear.

The Road to Latino Wealth

"Latino wealth is definitely emerging and will only grow over time. But it is not a community totally comfortable with wealth. That makes people less likely to seek advice that can limit their wealth creation."

- Haydee Caldero, co-founder Dignitas, LLC a private asset investment firm

In Haydee's opinion, the biggest thing we can do to build wealth in the Latino community is to understand that savings can be used to invest in opportunities that can grow over time. Over time, these investments multiply what one person is able to earn into what five people are able to earn, simply by the act of investing.

She believes that the way to incentivize savings is to write down your long-term goals and prioritize them, and then weigh what happiness this will provide you in comparison to something you can buy today that is really not a core need for you. So compare what it will be worth for you to retire earlier or pay for your kids' college versus buying that new car you would look great in.

Haydee advises people that if you can't afford to pay something basic without debt, you probably should not buy it. She has found that wealthy people typically only use debt for productive purposes, such as buying income-producing real estate. She also believes that you should NOT take on credit card debt.

Haydee has advised people from all walks of life, from policemen to lawyers to high-ranking executives, and she has learned that it is not what you make, but what you save and invest that leads to wealth.

Nely Galan, the super successful founder of the Adelante movement, is well known for providing the following advice to young Latinas: "Don't buy shoes, buy buildings." She pushes them to invest in things that will make them money and not shoes and purses that lose their value as soon as you walk out of the store where you bought them.

Buying things without long-term value hurts your ability to save and ultimately become wealthy.

Si Se Puede (*It is possible*)

"You can slowly and meticulously save money and create wealth so you can enjoy your grandkids when you retire"

- Ruben Rojas, the Entrepreneurs' Personal Financial Coach

It is very possible for you to build wealth in your lifetime even if you have nothing, even if you are making a low income, and even if you don't have connections.

Felix Montelara was making only $10K a year at age 30. One day he woke up and realized that his financial situation was unsustainable. He had four kids and a wife but he was living in a small, rented apartment, barely scraping by.

He thought about the sacrifices he had made emigrating from Puerto Rico and realized that he owed it to himself and his family to achieve his dream. So he dedicated himself to learning how to make more money, how to save, and how to invest. His goal became to make what he calls the "hardest million," which of course is the first one.

Seventeen years later, Felix became a millionaire. This is how he did it:

1. He understood that he needed to start with baby steps and that he might trip himself up in the process, but he was willing to do what it took to achieve his goals.

2. The first thing he did was increase his income; he got a new job in another area of the police department, which increased his income from $10K to $38K a year. This was a huge increase for him.

3. He devoted himself to learning how to become a millionaire. He read the book "*The Millionaire Next Door*" and from this book he learned that real millionaires don't spend to flaunt their money; instead, they saved.

4. He saved $10K a year for five years until he was able to buy his first home; he bought it with a good down payment, which gave him a low mortgage payment. The low payment allowed him to continue to save, so he did investing in his work's 401K. He benefitted from the amazing power of compounding to grow his wealth over the next twelve years.

5. To further increase his income, he started to earn more income on the side. He went into real estate, buying seven houses and renting them out to pay for the mortgages. He took on debt to buy these houses; he knew this was a risk, but he had good savings to protect him when the renters didn't come through with the rent on occasion. He managed to pay the mortgages in seven years by paying 3 extra payments every year, which allowed him to pay the principal faster and decreased the actual interest he ended up paying on his mortgages.

Felix's approach to becoming a millionaire is just one of many paths you can take to personal wealth and financial security. His story shows us that it doesn't matter how low your income is; you can become a millionaire by using the principles in this chapter:

- Increase your income.
- Get out of debt.
- Save as much as you can.
- Invest wisely to capitalize on the incredible power of compounding.

Felix shows people how he did it in his book *Potencial Millonario* in which he lays out his 11 golden rules that lead to becoming wealthy.

Generate Passive Income

Austin Netzley is the bestselling author of *Make Money, Live Wealthy* and was one of my first guests on the "Logra Tu Dream" podcast. He retired at age 27 from his corporate career when he achieved financial freedom.

Austin is also the founder of *Epic Launch*, a very successful self-publishing business in which he teaches people to write, publish, and make their book an Amazon bestseller.

He achieved financial freedom at an early age when his passive income surpassed his living expenses. He grew his passive income by investing heavily in the stock market while working for a corporation.

He then started a side business. The income he generated from his investments and his side business helped him build up a large fund of money. He had become wealthy and was able to retire at 27 to travel the world and gain complete freedom. With this freedom came piece of mind, confidence and happiness.

Financial freedom= Passive Income > Living Expenses

What is Passive Income?

Passive income is the ability to earn money without trading your time for it.

Passive income is when you make money in your sleep. It is not limited by the time you are able to work; it is limitless because it is based on an asset that is created once and generates income indefinitely.

How can this be possible, you might ask?

How Passive Income Works

You create or buy an asset that can generate money for you without you having to put in your time every time you sell it. It can be a service that you create once and you sell many times automatically without having to do anything.

It can be real estate which you buy and you rent, receiving income without having to do practically anything to generate it. It can be book that you write once and you earn money every times it sells without having to do any additional work.

Passive income is fantastic because it frees up your time while earning you money— sometimes, a lot of money. A number of successful online entrepreneurs have perfected the art of generating passive income. They have devised business models that generate passive income very successfully.

Here are some examples of very successful passive income machines that entrepreneurs I have interviewed on the "Logra Tu Dream" podcast have built:

Maritza Parra's List Building
Maritza has created a number of products over the last few years that help people grow their email lists and create products that generate significant money from that list of people. Maritza is an amazing entrepreneur and one of the top experts in building a large following and monetizing it.

Angelica Atondo
Angelica Atondo has built a loyal following/tribe based on her great work as Univision anchor, on her community service and engaging social media presence. She is the author of two books about how Latinos and Latinas can succeed in this country and maximize their potential.

Because she has built a very large following (100K+) of people who know, like and trust her, she has been able to sell thousands of copies of her books, generating a very nice source of passive income for her. Aside from her books, Angelica is the partner in a number of restaurant businesses from which she also generates passive income.

John Lee Dumas

When it comes to building passive income off a podcast platform, few people have been more successful at it than John Lee Dumas, the founder of Entrepreneur on Fire. After six months of growing the audience of his super successful podcast "Entrepreneur on Fire," he developed Podcasters Paradise, a community and online course to help people start, grow, and monetize their podcast.

John also generates passive income from a webinar course, his book, and a mastermind group. These businesses are highly automated, not requiring much of John's time, and they are generating more than $3 million a year just two years after he started them.

Action Steps

- ✓ Realize the power of compounding to build wealth
- ✓ Invest in yourself—your most important asset
- ✓ Avoid debt like the plague
- ✓ Follow Andres Gutierrez baby steps to financial freedom
- ✓ Save and invest your money to get compounding to work for you
- ✓ Generate passive income

Chapter 16

BUILD A LEGACY

"We cannot seek achievement for ourselves and forget about progress and prosperity for our community...Our ambitions must be broad enough to include the aspirations and needs of others, for their sakes and our own"

- Cesar Chavez

Create a Life of Meaning

I feel incredibly fortunate to be alive today.

To be able to enjoy the wonders of life and the moments that fill me with love, happiness, and awe.

I am grateful for every day that I am able to look into my precious children's eyes and realize how amazing, fleeting, and fragile the gift of life really is.

So what are we to do with this precious gift called life?

You only get to live once, for about 80 years on average. In these 80 years, what impact do you want to have in other people's lives?

What wonderful moments do you want to experience?

What do you want to be remembered for when you are no longer here?

What legacy do you want to leave your children and your community?

These are the big questions that have inspired me to find and pursue my purpose in life, to get on a path to create the life of my dreams and to work hard to leave a legacy...

I want to leave a legacy for my kids that they can draw upon so they can live the life of *their* dreams:

- A good example they can learn from
- The knowledge they need to succeed
- The values to be good people
- The financial foundation so they can have a good start
- Inspiration so that they, too can create a life of meaning and leave a legacy of their own.

I also want to leave a legacy to my community, a legacy of the knowledge and inspiration they can pursue to achieve their dreams. This is why I am writing this book; this book will outlive me and can inspire and help many people, many years after I am not around anymore.

Writing a book is a great way to leave a legacy and you can write your own book, too. Like Graciela Tiscareño Sato, who went from being an aviator in the Air Force to becoming a prominent Latina author. Graciela is leaving a legacy to our kids through her book, Captain Mama, a bilingual book for kids that explains why moms serve in the military.

I realized that, to leave a legacy, I must live a life of meaning. A life of meaning is one in which we contribute something that matters to the lives of others. What we contribute matters because it makes people's lives better, bringing happiness, freedom and fulfillment.

"Think about what you can do in your communities to achieve that common goal of supporting the Latino community to do more"

- *Maribel Duran, Chief of Staff, White House Initiative on Educational Excellence for Hispanics*

Maribel Duran is the Chief of Staff of the White House Initiative on Educational Excellence for Hispanics. She grew up in "La Villita," a working-class neighborhood in the heart of Chicago's Latino community. Her father worked at a plating company for 35 years, emigrating from Mexico in search of the American Dream.

Maribel's father instilled in her a deep appreciation for the value of education. He understood well the value of education, as he was only able to get a second grade education because he had to start working in the fields of Mexico when he was a little kid.

Through a lot of sacrifice, Maribel's parents provided her and her sister a private school education up to middle school. Then she was able to attend a great public school inside a business school, which required her to work at the same time in one of her fields of interest. She then became a consultant to public schools and discovered her passion for education.

"As Latinos, how do we engage others in seeing the value in investing in other Latinos?"

- Maribel Duran, Chief of Staff, White House Initiative on Educational Excellence for Hispanics

Having discovered her passion, Maribel set out to create a life of meaning, a life in which she could contribute to her community at the highest level in the field of education.

She now leads the White House's efforts to help disadvantaged Latinos and Latinas to achieve higher levels of education through a number of programs to improve early learning, STEM education, and high school graduation rates.

She never imagined that her path would lead her to work for the president of the United States. By the time she is done with her work at the White House Initiative, she will have helped millions of Latinos and Latinas secure a better education that will help them get farther in their lives.

Maribel will leave a strong legacy in her community because she has chosen to live a life of meaning.

Lead and inspire others behind you

Robert Renteria, the author of *From the Barrio to the Boardroom* and civic leader, has accomplished high levels of success in business, rising from an extremely difficult childhood. He overcame the absence of a father, poverty, gangs, drugs, and an abusive stepfather. He is now devoting his life to helping kids avoid gangs and develop the critical thinking skills they need to lead successful lives.

He is a regular keynote speaker in the Latino community who has impacted thousands, maybe even millions, of kids, not just in the US but across the world with his books. Robert has shown these kids that it is possible to overcome the worst adversities and the terrible influence of gangs to build happy and successful lives.

Robert is inspiring the kids he touches in his community and also other Latino leaders to follow his lead and do their part to help others behind them.

"I am being of service to the world, I am a messenger"

- Deborah Deras, life coach and speaker

Deborah Deras' passion has always been to empower the Hispanic community; she is an entrepreneur, a life coach, and a speaker. Deborah learned that the way to success could be found by focusing all her energy on making the people she serves successful instead of focusing solely on her own success. This practice helped make her coaching practice incredibly successful, so much so that she didn't need to do any marketing.

Deborah is an agent of transformation and sees her mission as being of service to others in the Latino community to help them achieve their dreams. She has helped many of her students and her You Tube channel audience members to become speakers, coaches and authors.

By sharing her dreams with her audience, she has provided them the example they need, inspiring them to take action and follow her lead. They see that she is making her dreams a reality and realize they can do it, too.

Give back to your community

Chef Ambrocio Gonzalez immigrated to the US with nothing but a dream only a few years ago. Today, he is a successful restaurant entrepreneur, owning five restaurants in the Chicago area, with more on the way. Not only has he succeeded in business, but he has also built a strong brand as a top Hispanic chef in the Chicago area.

Ambrocio hosts the TV show *Nuestra Cocina,* a program sponsored by Nuestro Queso, the company for which I lead the marketing department. I chose to work with Ambrocio instead of other chefs not only because of his talent as a chef but also because of his commitment to giving back to his community.

I wanted to find a brand ambassador who would embody the mission of Nuestro Queso, which is to give back to the Hispanic families that support their business.

I found that person in Ambrocio; he is a frequent presence at events that support the Hispanic community and at schools where he shares his story to inspire Latino kids. He also gives back through his restaurants and has supported people in need in the community.

Along with Angelica Atondo, he made the last few months of a young Latina mother who was batting with cancer much better by visiting her in the hospital, providing moral support, bringing her food, and by organizing a community of support around her through Facebook.

It is no coincidence that the Chicago Hispanic community loves Ambrocio and is fueling his success. They love him not just because he is a nice person and talented chef, but also because he gives back to them and shows he cares consistently.

Ambrocio is succeeding and is bringing his community along with him.

It is very important that you give back to your community as you achieve higher levels of success. The most successful people are in a position to help their community the most. If the most successful among us don't help others behind them, we will not be able to progress as a community the way we should. We will continue to struggle with less access to opportunities and lower levels of success than we are capable of achieving.

Julissa Arce went from selling funnel cakes to pay for college to becoming a star at Goldman Sachs, despite being undocumented. Through hard work and smarts, Julissa was able to excel in college and get a job at Goldman Sachs, the most prestigious investment bank in the world. She thrived at Goldman Sachs, making it to VP using the same determination that characterized her.

She was making hundreds of thousands of dollars a year, and continuing on this career path would make her a fortune, setting her for life. Yet she knew she was not working towards her mission.

She felt the strong pull of her calling—to help undocumented immigrants achieve an education and success in this country.

So she decided to do what very few people have the courage to do: she left a career that would bring her incredible wealth in order to give back to her community and pursue her mission.

Julissa left Goldman Sachs, becoming the director of development at Define American, an organization that uses the power of story to transcend politics and shift the conversation around citizenship. She also co-founded and is Chairman of the Ascend Educational Fund, a college scholarship and mentorship program for New York City immigrant students, regardless of their immigration status.

It is not only the right thing to give back; it is also smart to help others. Maribel, Robert, Deborah, Ambrocio, and Julissa, like all the other amazing Latinos and Latinas in this book, are all giving back to their communities and are all succeeding at the highest level. In fact, the more they give, the more they receive. So give and you, too, will succeed.

Time is precious so don't waste it

We only have about 80 years on average to live on this earth. Of these 80 years, we are either children, teenagers, very young adults (0-20) or seniors (65-80) for about 35 years. During these 35 years, we are either learning and developing, or we are towards the end of our lives and are either ill or retired.

That leaves us about 45 years of adult life (20 to 65) in which we can actively create and have an impact in this world. It seems like a lot of time but once you break it down it is not that much. In our twenties, we finish our schooling and explore what we want to do in our lives.

If we are lucky, we find our calling in this decade; if not, we continue to search in our thirties. By then, many of us have families and other obligations that make change more difficult.

If we are not on the path to our dreams by then, it becomes increasingly difficult to change courses at that point. In our forties, the chains that bind us to the current path become stronger as financial obligations increase, and our career and income reach its peak. We start to get older and don't have all the youthful energy we used to have; change seems even more difficult at this point. By our fifties, we don't have much time left and our energy is waning.

You get my point... what seems like an eternity to find your mission in life and create a life of meaning gets shorter and shorter as life goes on. The more time it takes you to get on the path to your dreams, the harder it gets.

So don't waste your time. Take action and build a legacy you can be proud of, one that you can leave to your kids and your community!

Action Steps

- ✓ Create a life of meaning
- ✓ Lead and inspire others behind you
- ✓ Give back to your community
- ✓ Life is short—don't waste your time
- ✓ Leave a legacy to your children and community
- ✓ Write a book

Chapter 17
CONCLUSION

"*Success is something you attract by the person you become*"

-Jim Rohn

In this book I have synthesized the 12 proven principles 50 successful Latinos and Latinas use to turn their dreams into reality. Here is a summary of each of the principles that will help you to put it all together. The combination of the 12 principles amounts to a system of success which you can use as a roadmap to turn your dreams into reality:

1. BELIEVE THAT "SI SE PUEDE" (IT IS POSSIBLE)

It is hard to believe what we can't see. To believe in something, we need to see it first.

One of the biggest barriers standing in the way of the dreams of millions of Latinos and Latinas in this country is the lack of belief that they can be successful.

But when we are exposed to the stories of successful Latinos and Latinas, then we believe that it *is* possible.

We believe because we realize that others like us, with similar backgrounds, have been able to overcome the same barriers we face. So believe that it is possible and you will be able to turn your dreams into reality.

2. HAVE A BIG DREAM FOR YOUR LIFE

Dreaming big or small takes the same effort. Your dreams (thoughts) turn into beliefs, beliefs turn into actions, and actions turn into habits.

So if you dream small, that is what you will get. So why dream small?

Go Big and never let anyone tell you that you can't achieve them. Many people you'll read about in this book started in the worse possible situations and faced the toughest adversity, but they have accomplished their big dreams and so can you.

3.   BE GRATEFUL

Being grateful for what you have puts you in a state of mind that creates attitudes that will attract opportunities and the right people to your life.

All of the 50 successful Latinos and Latinas featured in this book are incredibly grateful people. They make a point of expressing gratitude to the people who help them, and they take time to reflect on what they are grateful for in their lives.

It is clear that gratitude is a very important factor of their success. So be grateful; not just because it is the right thing to do, but because it will fuel your success.

4.   EMBRACE THE ABUNDANCE MINDSET

One of the biggest challenges holding back Latino success in America is the scarcity mindset. When I asked my guests about the biggest barriers we face in our community, this has come up again and again.

We need to adopt a mindset of abundance because this is the mindset that works to achieve success. All of the successful people I have interviewed share this abundance mindset, as do the most successful people in the world like Warren Buffett, Tony Robbins, Charlie Munger, and others.

We need to realize that by helping each other, we will all be more successful. This is the way we get ahead; we gain nothing by taking down fellow Latinos and Latinas. We lift ourselves by lifting each other up.

5.   INVEST IN YOURSELF TO BECOME A LEARNING MACHINE

The best investment you can ever make is in yourself. The ability to learn, to adapt, and to master your domain is the most important skill you need to craft a life of success.

229

It is critical that you embrace the love of learning and become a lifelong reader if you want to be successful. I don't know successful people who don't read. Reading nurtures your mind and your soul. Your mind and soul need high-quality food, just like your body. Great books are great mind and soul foods.

Recognize that we can always improve by learning and practicing. Learn how to think, not what to think.

Learn how to pay for college without debt, avoid getting in debt for a degree the market will not reward, and when in doubt, choose full rides over prestigious schools if the latter means going into debt.

6. TAKE MASSIVE ACTION

You need to take massive action to turn your dream into reality. Break down your big dream into smaller goals you can achieve to make your huge dream possible, and then take massive action.

Action is critical because it gets you in the stream. You can't swim towards your next destination if you are standing outside the water. You need to get in the water and start swimming; very soon, you'll be in the stream with other people and the resources you need to get ahead. Hustle like your life depended on it and you'll get what you want.

7. GET MENTORED

The main barrier to achieving the American Dream in the Latino community is the lack of Latino & Latina mentors and the lack of mentorship from them.

You need to get mentored because being able to learn through somebody else's experience saves you years of hard knocks and failure.

This is why the most successful Latinos & Latinas, along with the most successful people in the world, have mentors and why you should find mentors, too.

8.   BE A GIVER & SURROUND YOURSELF WITH PEOPLE WHO PULL YOU UP

Nobody succeeds alone. Throughout my own life and across my conversations with more than 50 successful Latinos and Latinas, I noticed that every one of them has surrounded themselves with the right people. So surround yourself with people who will pull you up. These people are givers and they will help you get what you want.

BUT to be able to attract givers to your life, who will support you in your journey, you must yourself be a giver.

So build your network by helping others, being authentic, and proactively connecting with key people in your field. Build meaningful relationships with your network based on trust, respect, and reciprocity.

9.   BRING YOUR UNIQUE VALUE TO MARKETPLACE

Think for yourself and see reality for what it really is, as this is how you will find your uniqueness and mission. To find your uniqueness, you must find your strengths and identify your mission.

To do this, you first need to listen more to your gut and capture what you are learning about yourself. Once you find

231

your strengths, build on them by putting in the reps, as you can't be the best at something that doesn't leverage your biggest strengths.

10.   MASTER THE ONE THREAD YOU CAN DO BETTER THAN ANYBODY ELSE

This ONE thread is the unique combination of these factors that will differentiate you from others and what you will need to become a master at. Weave and master the ONE thread that connects and combines your mission and your unique set of skills, talents, experiences, and work.

Find a problem you deeply desire to solve and fill the gap. Experiment your way to success. Be persistent and practice, practice, practice until you master your niche.

11.   BECOME A CREATOR, NOT A CONSUMER

Make a decision to pursue your dream. Realize that being a consumer doesn't build your dream but somebody else's dream so create something of value for yourself.
Look for ways you might be able to capitalize on the Latino market opportunity. Figure out what is the right path for you that aligns with your mission, existing & future skills and knowledge.

Build your platforms and either go all in or make time for side hustling (turn off the TV). Read this book again, focusing on the sections of surrounding yourself with the right people, getting mentored, mastering the ONE thread you can do better than anybody else, building a network, building a platform, and taking massive action.

12.   COMPOUNDING

Compounding is one of the most powerful forces in life because, over time, it turns very small gains into huge ones. Realize the power of compounding to build wealth, and then invest in yourself and master your craft to create a compound effect in your career and your business.

Avoid debt like the plague by following Andres Gutierrez baby steps to financial freedom. Save and invest your money to get compounding to work for you and generate passive income to become financially free.

A Call to Action to All Latinos & Latinas!

Whether you aspire to start or grow an entrepreneurial business, achieve success in your career pursuing your passion, or build wealth to a secure a better future for our families, by reading this book you now have the roadmap you need to turn your dreams into reality.

If you embrace the principles of success I've laid out in this book, you will create the life that you want and secure a better future for your family.

I wrote this book because I wanted to share the principles I discovered successful Latinos & Latinas are using to achieve their success so you don't have to make all the mistakes that will set you back in your journey.

When I started my journey, I didn't find a roadmap of how other Latinos were succeeding in the US, but now I have found it and shared it with you.

The next step is up to you.

The key is to take action; take the first step and believe that it is possible for you to achieve your dreams. Make a commitment to yourself that you will work very hard to turn your dreams into reality.

If Raymmar Tirado can go from college dropout who could not find real work to founder of Raymmar.com, which has over 3.5 million page views, so can you.

If Robert Renteria was able to rise from the barrio to the boardroom and to bestselling author, overcoming gangs, drugs and the absence of a father, so can you.

If Gaby Natale can go from unemployed graduate in Argentina to president of her own successful media company in the US in just a few years, so can you.

You will have to work very hard but know that the rewards will far outweigh all the sacrifice.

I created the Logra Tu Dream podcast and wrote this book to help you empower yourself to reach for and achieve your potential.

I envision a future in which we are empowered by the strength of our culture and much more widely recognized by the mainstream for our talents, achievements, and tremendous contributions to our society.

After all, there are already 54 million of us living in the US; we represent 60 percent of US population growth. Latinos are forecasted to be 30 percent of US population by 2060.

Latino culture offers some of the most fascinating, beautiful, and flavorful inspiration in the world. It is also having a tremendous influence on mainstream America, which is adopting Latin-inspired food, music, products, and culture at a rapid rate.

Across industries, companies are investing billions to persuade us to buy their products and services.

Yet despite all this, we are often portrayed in a stereotypical manner, ignored by the mainstream media or sometimes even insulted and belittled by ignorant and intolerant elements of our society.

Our time has come to raise our voices to show the world the beauty of our culture, the talent of our people, and the depth of our soul.

Our time has come to empower ourselves to take deliberate and massive action that will bring us closer to creating the life we want.

Our time has come to fulfill our great promise.

Our future is bright and our dreams are within reach if we decide to pursue them.

I would love to know what your dreams are and to hear from you on what the #1 barrier is that stands between you and making your dreams a reality.

I am building a community where you can find the support and encouragement you need to achieve your success, and where you can help others achieve theirs.

You picked this book for a reason. It inspired your interest because you share the aspiration to create the life of your dreams. It is now your turn to take action.

Although you might now understand all the key principles you need to use, you may be looking for more help.

This is why I am thinking about creating an online course based on the material in this book. The program would offer in-depth information, tools and step-by-step instructions on what you are more interested in learning about from this book.

The program would also provide you access to a community of like-minded people who will support you, encourage you and hold you accountable so that you can create the change you want in your life.

Please let me know which principles in this book you would like to learn more about in the survey here: www.logratudream.com/survey. Also please feel free to reach me at Arturo@logratudream.com with your feedback.

If you are serious about pursuing your highest aspirations, you need to take massive action. I hope that you will send me a note when you put in to action what you learned in this book, telling me how you are doing and how your life has changed for the better.

Together, we can make this movement as inspiring and actionable as it can be. I invite you to sign up to the podcast at www.logratudream.com, www.logratudream.com/itunes on iTunes, or www.logratudream.com/Android on Android, where you'll find more inspiration and mentorship that will help you get closer to your dreams.

Please join me in this important journey.

Keep the Fire in your belly burning and you will Logra Tu Dream!!

Arturo Nava

ABOUT THE AUTHOR

Arturo Nava is a Brand Builder, Author and Founder of Logra Tu Dream a #1 Amazon bestselling book and top podcast in a mission to help Latinos & Latinas achieve their American Dream.

Arturo has interviewed more than 50 of the most inspiring and influential Latinos, Latinas and Latin-inspired entrepreneurs and leaders on Logra Tu Dream. He was inspired to write this book by the stories of people like Gaby Natale the president of Super Latina TV, Deldelp Medina Founder of Avion Ventures, Manny Ruiz the founder of Hispanicize and many other amazing people who have overcome obstacles to turn their dreams into reality.

Arturo was born and raised in Mexico City and came to the US in the late nineties to follow his American Dream to build better life and start a family. His ticket to his new life in the

237

US came via his acceptance to the MBA program at Harvard and via scholarship he won to finance his studies.

Once in the US, Arturo became an entrepreneur and brand builder. After his first venture didn't work, he spent 13 years marketing top brands in the Latino and General Market at Fortune-500 companies like P&G, MillerCoors and Marketealo, his own consulting firm. He is currently the Marketing Director of Nuestro Queso, an Illinois Hispanic dairy company.

After living in the US for more than 18 years, he was deeply inspired by the stories of struggle and triumph of many Latinos and Latinas who are pursuing their dreams of a better life for their families. He saw that many times standing in the way of their dreams was a lack of access to inspiration, mentorship and business coaching from successful Latino and Latina role models.

Arturo realized that his mission was to do his part in helping other Latinos achieve their dreams. So he decided to start the Logra Tu Dream podcast in which successful Latinos and Latinas share their stories to inspire and mentor Latinos and Latinas to help them get closer to their dreams.

His biggest blessings are his two precious kids, his close knit family, his loving girlfriend, his good friends and good health.

His definition of success: "The ability to be able to do what makes you happy."

Want to know more?

Check out his podcast at www.Logratudream.com, a growing platform for Latinos and Latinas in pursuit of their dreams.

Twitter: @logratudream (www.twitter.com/logratudream)

Facebook: www.facebook.com/logratudream

BOOK ARTURO TO SPEAK

Book Arturo as your next keynote speaker (in English or Spanish) and you are assured to inspire your team/group to take massive action to turn their dreams into reality.

Arturo has synthesized what he has learned from the most successful Latinos & Latinas in the nation into the 12 principles framework that is creating breakthroughs in peoples' lives. Aside from speaking about the principles in this book he also speaks on how to start and grow your podcast, how to create your brand and build your platform and how to win in the Latino market.

Arturo's authenticity and passion allow him to relate to his audience at a level most can't, which is why he has inspired thousands of people through his podcasts and speaking engagements to take action to get closer to their dreams.

*"A Champion for Latino Success! Having witnessed Logra Tu Dream rise from Idea to Podcast to Publication, the evolution of the author's desire to give back to the community by highlighting inspirational stories of successes in individuals own words has been a fantastic journey in itself. The wisdom and stories from members of our community working to achieve goals, build businesses, transcend challenges and barriers are motivational for anyone looking to begin any new endeavor. Achieve your dreams."- **Mahrinah von Schlegel, Global Innovation and Strategy Consultant, Entrepreneur and Investor***

For more information visit:
www.logratudream.com/speaking
Or contact Arturo directly at: arturo@logratudream.com

RESOURCES

Tests

- Strengths Finder 2.0 book and evaluation

Books

- Zero to One, Peter Thiel
- The E-Myth Revisited, Michael Gerber
- Essentialism, Greg Mckeown
- The Alchemist, Paulo Coelho
- Meditations, Marcus Aurelius
- The ONE Thing, Gary Keller
- Poor Charlie's Almanac, Charlie Munger
- Choose Yourself, James Altucher
- The Art of Being Unmistakable, Srinvas Rao
- The Richest Man in Babylon, George S. Clason
- Think and Grow Rich, Napoleon Hill
- Man's Search for Meaning, Victor Frankl
- Total Recall, Arnold Schwarzenegger
- Mindset, Carol Dweck
- The Selfish Gene, Richard Dawkins
- The Miracle Morning, Hal Elrod
- Bold, Peter Diamandis
- The Millionaire Next Door, Thomas J. Stanley
- Launch, Jeff Walker
- Give and Take, Adam Grant
- Money Master the Game, Tony Robbins
- Smartcuts, Shane Snow
- The 4-Hour work week, Tim Ferris
- The Total Money Makeover, Dave Ramsey
- Rich Dad, Poor Dad, Robert Kyosaki
- How to Win Friends and Influence People, Dale Carnegie

- Managing Oneself, Peter Drucker
- The Compound Effect, Darren Hardy
- Lessons of History, Will and Ariel Durant
- Crush it , Gary Vaynerchuk
- Jab, Jab, Jab, Right Hook, Gary Vaynerchuk
- Outliers, Malcolm Gladwell
- The Millionaire Messenger, Brendon Bruchard
- Mastery, Robert Greene
- The Success Principles, Jack Canfield

Online Education Platforms

- **Audible:** www.logratudream.com/audible
- www.udemy.org
- www.coursera.org
- **iTunes University:**
  www.logratudream.com/itunesuniversity

Logra Tu Dream Podcast Interviews with Successful Latinos & Latinas

You can find all the Logra Tu Dream interviews at: www.logratudream.com/podcasts. Here is a list of all the great people that I interviewed most of whom you will find featured in this book:

- Gaby Natale
- Nely Galan
- Deborah Deras
- Jorge Narvaez
- Julissa Arce
- Felix Montelara
- Sandra Alfaro

- Andres Gutierrez
- Cristian Arcega
- Angelica Atondo
- Hipatia Lopez
- Maribel Duran
- Fernanda Chacon
- Fidel Vargas
- Ray Collazo
- Alex Torrenegra
- Marissa Fernandez
- Esteban Arias
- Kyra Caruso
- Tanya Salcido
- Lizza Monet Morales
- Luis De la Hoz
- Ambrocio Gonzalez
- Komal Dadlani
- Jackie Camacho
- Manny Ruiz
- Raymmar Tirado
- Camilo Anabalon
- Judith Duval
- Sonia Farace
- Deldelp Medina
- Erick "Roho" Garcia
- Edrizio de La Cruz
- Robert Renteria
- Mariana Ferrari
- Ruben Rojas
- Tayde Aburto

- Gianpaolo Pietri
- Fernando Labastida
- Jesse Martinez
- Haydee Caldero
- Toby Salgado
- Felix Ortiz
- Mahrinah Von Schlegel
- Pablo Fuentes
- Jose Huitron
- Maritza Parra
- Mauricio Simbeck
- Cynthia Sanchez
- David Gomez
- Grace Tiscareño Sato
- Marcie Quintana
- Claudia Espinosa

Logra Tu Dream Podcast Interviews with Successful Latin- Inspired Entrepreneurs

- Austin Netzley
- Gary Vaynerchuk
- Chris Cummings
- Chris Brogan
- Celest Horton
- John Lee Dumas
- Michael O'Neal
- Michael Kawula
- David Chitel

I am incredibly grateful to all the Logra Tu Dream podcast guests!!

Audio Book Recording

- Eddie Torres Music: www.eddietorresmusic.wix.com/eddietorres

Cover Designer

- Juan Correa: http://juancorreacreative.blogspot.com/

References

1. 2011 study of business owners and entrepreneurs conducted by GfK Custom Research North America for Massachusetts Mutual Life Insurance Company.
2. Andrés Gutiérrez: www.andresgutierrez.com
3. Education Pays 2013, The Benefits of Higher Education for Individuals and Society.
4. 2014 Gallup's State of the American Workplace study.
5. www.Marketealo.com
6. Latina Power Shift- Nielsen 2013

THE LOGRA TU DREAM 12 PRINCIPLES FRAMEWORK

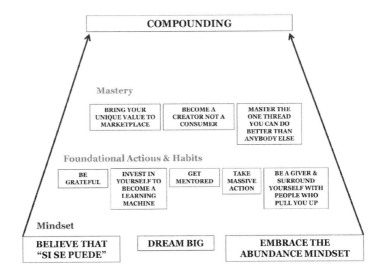

246

Before You Go

If you got something out of this book, if you took notes, if it shifted your thinking, or inspired you I am hoping you'll do this for me:

Give a copy to somebody you care about, ask them to read it, let them know it is possible to turn their dreams into reality if they believe, have "ganas" (hustle), and decide to take massive action. We need them and we need you.

Please spread the word.

Thank you!

I NEED YOUR HELP!

Thank you for buying and reading my book!

It means a lot to me that you took time to read this book. If you liked it and it was helpful to you, could you PLEASE leave a review on Amazon?

Just go to www.logratudream.com/amazonreview to leave me a helpful review on Amazon, letting me know what you thought of the book.

Thank you for your support!!

~Arturo Nava

Made in the USA
San Bernardino, CA
27 May 2016